Tank driver: with the 11th Armored
BIOG Hartman **T38336**

DATE DUE

MAR 0 4 2014		
MAR 1 1 2014		
MAR 2 2 2014		
JUN - 3 2014 *IVL*		
FEB 2 1 2017 *NF*		
JUN 1 7 2017		
DEC 2 8 2018		
		PRINTED IN U.S.A.

TANK DRIVER

TANK DRIVER

With the 11th Armored from the Battle of the Bulge to VE Day

J. TED HARTMAN

INDIANA
University Press

Bloomington & Indianapolis

This book is a publication of
Indiana University Press
601 North Morton Street
Bloomington, IN 47404-3797 USA

http://iupress.indiana.edu

Telephone orders   800-842-6796
Fax orders   812-855-7931
Orders by e-mail   iuporder@indiana.edu

The paper used in this publication meets the minimum requirements of American National Stan-
dard for Information Sciences—Permanence of Paper for Printed Library Materials, ANSI Z39.48-
1984.

Manufactured in the United States of America

Library of Congress Cataloging-in-Publication Data

Hartman, J. Ted, date
  Tank driver : with the 11th Armored from the Battle of the Bulge to VE
Day / J. Ted Hartman.
    p. cm.
Includes bibliographical references and index.
  ISBN 0-253-34211-2 (alk. paper)
  1. Hartman, J. Ted, date 2. World War, 1939–1945—
Personal narratives, American. 3. World War, 1939–1945—
Tank warfare. 4. World War, 1939–1945—Campaigns—
Western Front. I. Title.
  D811.H346 A3 2003
  940.54'21'092—dc21

2002151518

1 2 3 4 5 08 07 06 05 04 03

Dedicated to the memory of my buddies
of Company B, 41st Tank Battalion
who did not come home

CONTENTS

MAPS

FOREWORD

When J. Ted Hartman became a driver in an M4 Sherman tank in the 11th Armored Division, he joined a relatively new branch of the U.S. Army. While the army was forward-looking in certain areas before World War II, this was not the case with tanks or armor tactics. In 1919, in the drawdown of U.S. forces following World War I, the Tank Corps was abolished. The National Defense Act the next year assigned the tanks to the infantry, consistent with army belief that tanks should support attacking infantry.

In 1927 the army set up the small experimental Mechanized Force of light tanks, but in 1931 Chief of Staff General Douglas MacArthur decreed that tanks would have an exploitation role apart from infantry support, and the cavalry took over the Mechanized Force. In order to get around the 1920 Defense Act, however, the tanks were known as "combat cars."

The German employment of armor divisions in the September 1939 German invasion of Poland, and especially in the May–June 1940 defeat of France, dramatically changed the U.S. Army's attitude toward tanks and their role. In April 1940 an improvised U.S. armored division, formed of the mechanized 7th Cavalry Brigade from Fort Knox, Kentucky, and the Provisional Tank Brigade from Fort Benning, Georgia, dominated the army's Louisiana maneuvers. In July the army created the U.S. Armored Force, led by Brigadier General Adna Romanaza Chaffee Jr., to test the feasibility of tank divisions. In July 1943 the Armored Force was redesignated the Armored Command, and in February 1944 it became the Armored Center.

The armor division was the basic element of the Armored Force. In 1941 the U.S. Army postulated that to win a war against Germany and Japan, it would be necessary to raise 215 maneuver divisions, of which 61 were to be armored. The army ended the war fielding only 89 divisions, of which only 16 were armored. As it turned out, this smaller number of divisions was sufficient to bring victory. These divisions were the most heavily armed, mechanized, and maneuverable to that point in history.

The U.S. armored division was designed to be a self-sufficient combined arms organization, capable of rapid movement and penetration deep into an enemy's rear areas. The old heavy foot-bound four-brigade divisions of World War I gave way to a triangular system based on three highly mobile brigades. The triangular concept continued down through the unit of one maneuver element to hold an enemy in place, another maneuver element to turn its flank, and a third maneuver element in reserve. This same concept applied to the new armored divisions.

In 1943 the sixteen armored divisions were reorganized, and all except the 2d and 3d "heavy" divisions were converted into "light" divisions. Each had three tank battalions, and each of these, in turn, had one light and three medium tank companies. In the case of Hartman's 11th Armored Division, the three battalions were the 22d, the 41st (the author's unit was Company B of this battalion), and the 42d. The 11th Armored also had a field artillery regiment (consisting of the 490th, 491st, and 492d Battalions) and a reconnaissance element (the 41st Cavalry Reconnaissance Squadron). Division support consisted of an armored infantry regiment (the 21st, 55th, and 63d Armored Infantry Battalions), a tank destroyer battalion (three different ones in the course of the division's existence), and the 575th Antiaircraft Battalion. The division also had the service elements of the 56th Armored Engineer Battalion, the 81st Medical Battalion, the 133d Ordnance Maintenance Battalion, the 151st Signal Company, and a military police platoon. Authorized personnel strength was quite lean: 10,937 men. New tables of January 1945 added nine additional medium tanks to each division but reduced the personnel further, to 10,670.

Division equipment under the 1945 table of organization included 268 medium tanks, 77 light tanks, 54 armored cars, 451 halftracks, 18 105mm howitzer tanks, 449 ¼-ton trucks ("jeeps"), 77 ¾-ton trucks, 444 2½-ton ("deuce-and-a-half") trucks, 40 other trucks, 30 tank recovery vehicles, and 8 liaison aircraft.

The basic armored division light tank was the M5 "General Stuart" with twin Cadillac automobile engines. Originally to be the Light Tank M4, it was designated the M5 to avoid confusion with the M4 medium "Sherman" tank, then entering production. Recognizable by its stepped-up rear deck, the General Stuart had a crew of four, a weight of 16.5 tons, maximum 67mm armor, and armament of 1 × 37mm gun and 2 × .30 caliber machine guns.

With only a 37mm gun, the M5 was hopelessly outgunned by its opponents. The M24 "Chaffee" answered the need for a light tank with heavier armament. Entering production in March 1944 and reaching units in the field in late 1944, this highly successful design was manufactured in a variety of models. The 20-ton M24 had a crew of five and maximum 38mm armor, and mounted a 75mm gun and three machine guns: 2 × .30 caliber (1 coaxial) and 1 × .50 caliber.

The medium tank utilized by the U.S. armored divisions was the M4 Sherman. Produced in a considerable variety of models, it was certainly the most widely used Allied tank of the war. In all, some 49,000 were manufactured. The M4 continued in service after the war and was later used extensively by the Israeli Army.

The M4 utilized the lower hull of the M3 with a redesigned upper hull, mounting a central turret with a 75mm gun. It weighed 33 tons, had a crew of five and maximum 51mm armor, and mounted a 75mm main gun and 1 × .50 caliber and 2 × .30 caliber machine guns. The Sherman first saw service in North Africa in 1942. It had two great advantages over the German tanks: its powered turret enabled crews to react and fire more quickly; and it had greater mechanical reliability and repairability. Rugged, maneuverable, and easy to maintain, the M4 was consistently upgraded in main gun and armor during the course of the war.

The Sherman's great disadvantages were its engine and main gun. Its gasoline (vice diesel) engine earned it the GI nickname of "Ronson Lighter—lights first time every time." The Sherman was also consistently outgunned by the larger German tanks against which it had to fight. As Hartman notes, its 75mm gun was relatively ineffective against German armor, but a replacement 76mm gun with much higher muzzle velocity helped rectify that. The British were the first to use the 76mm gun on their Shermans, which they called the Sherman Firefly; the Americans soon followed suit with the heavier gun.

One of the major problems for the U.S. Army in the war was the lack of a heavy tank. German tanks had thicker frontal armor and a much higher velocity gun. Their "Tiger" mounted an 88mm. The 88mm German *Panzerschreck* anti-tank weapon could easily knock out the Shermans, whereas the U.S. 2.36" Bazooka, from which it was copied, was effective only against German side armor. Also, the Sherman tread mark was only 14", while German tanks had a track twice as wide and thus were not as easily bogged down. Indeed, Hartman describes adding extensions to his tank track just before the Battle of the Bulge in order to rectify this situation.

Loss rates of Sherman tanks were simply staggering. In the course of 1944–1945 the 3d Armored Division alone lost 648 M4s completely destroyed in combat and another 700 knocked out, repaired, and put back into operation—a loss rate of 580 percent. In fact, the U.S. lost 6,000 tanks in Europe in World War II. The Germans never had more than half that total.

The answer to the German tanks, the M26 "Pershing" heavy tank, was not available until after the December 1944–January 1945 Battle of the Bulge. It was not available in large numbers earlier in part because influential Lieutenant General George S. Patton Jr. insisted on concentrating on high production of M4 Shermans since the Army needed a fast, medium tank, and because he believed that "tanks do not fight other tanks." Patton counted on tank destroyers to protect the U.S. tanks, but the M10 Wolverine tank destroyer of 1942 had only a 76mm gun. The M36 Jackson, introduced in 1944, had a 90mm gun, which could indeed take on the German Panthers and Tigers on an equal footing. Both the M10 and M36 used the Sherman chassis.

The Battle of the Bulge revealed the weakness of the M4 against heavy German tanks and led to the prompt shipment to Europe of the first M26 Pershings, the prototypes of which had been produced only in November 1944. Weighing 46 tons, the M26 had a crew of five, maximum 102mm (4") armor, and a 90mm gun, along with 1 × .50 caliber and 2 × .30 caliber machine guns. The muzzle velocity of its main gun did not match the 88mm German tank gun, but it was almost a match for the fearsome Tiger in firepower and surpassed it in terms of reliability and mobility. The M26 was not available to the 11th Armored Division. It was utilized only by the 3d and 9th Armored Divisions, from February 1945.

The 11th Armored Division was activated at Camp Polk, Louisiana, on 15 August 1942. Its first commander was Major General Edward H. Brooks. Transferred to Camp Barkeley, Texas, in September 1943, the division participated in maneuvers at the Desert Training Center in California that October and was stationed at Camp Cooke, California, in February 1944. The next month Brigadier General Charles S. Kilburn replaced Brooks as the division commander. At Camp Cooke Hartman joined the division, received his tank training, and was assigned as an M4 driver.

The 11th Division staged for overseas deployment at Camp Kilmer, New Jersey, in September 1944. At the end of that month it embarked from the port of New York for Liverpool, England, where it arrived two weeks later. In England the division was assigned to Camp Tilshead, on the Salisbury Plain. After getting its equipment in order, the division trained for six weeks. The 11th Armored Division departed from England, arriving at Cherbourg beginning on 17 December. Hartman's company of eighteen tanks left Weymouth on LSTs on 19 December and arrived at Cherbourg two days later. A week later the division was engaged in the largest land battle ever for U.S. troops.

The hope nourished by the Western Allies of winning the war in 1944 had vanished in their failure to close the Falaise-Argentan Gap, Field Marshal Bernard Montgomery's refusal to secure the Scheldt River, and the lack of success of the September Market-Garden Operation, whereby Montgomery sought to outflank the German Siegfried Line (called the West Wall by the Germans) by securing a crossing point over the lower Rhine at Arnhem. In December, when Hartman arrived in France, Allied armies were regrouping, expecting to soon resume the offensive. Indeed, Hartman's division was slotted to be sent to southern France.

Allied forces in the Ardennes area were weak, as Supreme Allied commander General Dwight D. Eisenhower had deployed most of his strength northward and southward. Hitler now gambled on a last throw of the dice. His goal was to smash through the Allied lines, cut off a sizable portion of their forces, and seize the port of Antwerp. In an exceptional achievement, the Germans assembled 250,000 men, 1,420 tanks and assault guns, and 1,920 rocket and artillery pieces, along with 2,000 planes.

The German Ardennes Offensive, launched early on 16 December, took the Allies completely by surprise. The Allies had grown complacent; their intelligence had failed to detect the German buildup, and they assumed that only they could launch an offensive. Bad weather favored the attackers by restricting the use of Allied air power.

Eisenhower now called up all available reserves, including the 11th Armored Division. The German force of twenty-four divisions pushing against three divisions of Lieutenant General Courtney Hodges' First Army soon drove a "bulge" in the American defenses, which gave the battle its name. The German penetration eventually extended fifty miles deep and seventy miles wide.

On 23 December the 11th Armored Division was ordered up to the Givet-Sedan sector in reserve in direct response to the German offensive. Hartman's unit arrived at Soissons on Christmas Eve. Here he learned that the 11th Armored had been assigned to General Patton's Third Army.

Hartman's unit then moved to near Sedan, where the German panzers had broken through in the Battle for France in May 1940. On 29 December the author's company moved to the vicinity of Neufchâteau, Belgium, and early the next morning it joined the Battle of the Bulge, attacking against strong German opposition toward Houffalize. The 11th Division was without its artillery, which had been delayed in traffic jams and bad weather, and the tankers suffered heavy losses in the attack. Two of the eighteen tanks in Hartman's company were knocked out, and thirteen crewmen were killed, including his company commander, and others wounded. It was a rude awakening for young Hartman, who was seeing his first combat. The division did take its objective of Lavaselle, and that night it repulsed a German counterattack.

The next day Hartman's tank participated in two attacks by the 11th Armored on Chenogne, both of which were driven back. On 1 January 1945, supported by artillery and air power, the division took Chenogne and pushed past it ten miles toward Mande St. Étienne. The next day, in fierce fighting, the tankers took that place, although Hartman's acting company commander was wounded and had to be evacuated.

On 3 January the division was relieved by the 17th Airborne Division and sent back to Bercheux, Belgium, to rest and refit. After nine days it returned to the line. On 14 January, Hartman's company struck north and helped retake Foy, which had been captured by the Germans the night before. It then moved on Noville. In the fighting for Noville, Hartman's company lost seven of its twelve tanks, including Hartman's own M4, which was disabled. His replacement tank was one of the up-gunned 76mm Shermans. Part of the 11th Armored Division reached Villeroux on 15 January but was pushed back by a German counterattack. The next day it took Villeroux. On 18 January the division took over the Hardigny-Bourcy line, and two days later began advancing after German withdrawals. It crossed the Luxembourg border on 22 January and then patrolled in the vicinity of Bois de Rouvroy.

By the end of January, the U.S. First and Third Armies had reached the German frontier and reestablished the front of just six weeks before. The Battle of the Bulge was over. Of 600,000 U.S. troops involved, 19,000 were killed, about 47,000 were wounded, and 15,000 were prisoners. Among 55,000 British engaged, casualties totaled 1,400, of whom 200 were killed. The Germans, employing nearly 500,000 men in the battle, suffered nearly 100,000 casualties killed, wounded, and captured. Both sides suffered heavy equipment losses, about 800 tanks on each side, and the Germans lost virtually all their aircraft committed. But the Western Allies could easily make good their losses in a short period of time, while the Germans could not do so.

Although German defenses were crumbling, much hard fighting lay ahead, as Hartman was to discover when British and American forces came up against the German defensive line of the Siegfried Line. The 11th Armored now took part in the campaign to secure the Rhineland, the German territory west of the Rhine River. Although Hartman was in reserve in Binsfeld for almost a month, elements of his division relieved the 90th Infantry Division east of the Our River, and on 6 February assaulted the Siegfried Line and were repulsed. On the 18th a surprise assault without artillery preparation enabled the division to take numerous German pillboxes, and by the next day its units had taken Herzfeld and the Leidenborn area. Sengrich fell to the division on the 20th, and

Roscheid on the 21st. The next day Eschfeld and Reiff were captured. The division then consolidated its positions.

On 18 February U.S. infantry attacked the Siegfried Line without preliminary artillery fire, surprising the German defenders and allowing a path to be cleared for the tanks, although this task took several weeks. At the end of February, the 11th Armored Division renewed its forward movement. On 1 March it crossed the Our River and entered Germany, then halted west of Prüm, while engineers bridged that river. The division then crossed the river and took Prüm with little resistance. On 3 March it attacked through 4th Infantry Division lines toward the Kyll River, reaching it the next day near Lissigen.

On 6 March elements of the division crossed the Kyll. The next day the division took Kelberg after fierce fighting, and on 9 March, after a forty-eight-hour marathon drive, it reached the Rhine at Andernach and Burgbrohl. The division then mopped up and went into reserve.

General Holmes E. Dager took command of the division in March. On the 17th the division attacked through the Bullay Bridgehead of the 89th Infantry Division in its second drive to the Rhine, at Worms, entering that city with the 89th on the 22nd. Two days later the 11th relieved the 4th Armored Division in the Oppenheim-Worms sector of the Rhine and went into defensive positions.

After crossing the Rhine River at Oppenheim, the 11th moved up to the Main River at Hanau on 28 March. The next day the division advanced northeast toward Fulda. It took Gelnhausen on 30 March, and here Hartman's tank was hit by a *Panzerfaust* projectile. The division then bypassed Fulda, which was taken by the 71st Infantry Division, and pushed to the Werra River, establishing a bridgehead there on 1 April. For much of this time the 11th Armored Division moved at thirty miles a day or more into Germany.

The division took Coburg on 11 April, and the next day it resumed the offensive, establishing bridgeheads across the Hasslach River at Kronach and Marktzeuln. On 14 April it took Bayreuth, and on the 19th, Grafenwohr, the Wehrmacht armored center. Renewing the offensive on 22 April, it drove to the Naab River, then along the Alpine Highway to take Regen in fierce fighting on the 24th. Division elements struck south on 29 April, taking Wegscheid on the

Austrian border in heavy fighting on 30 April. The next day Hartman's 41st Battalion was in the lead as the division crossed into Austria, probably the first U.S. troops to do so. The division then secured the Urfahr-Linz complex on 5 May. Three days later, on 8 May, the day of the German formal surrender, it linked up with the Soviet Army at Amstetten. Hartman noted that an odometer on one of his Company B's halftracks indicated that the division had logged 1,000 combat miles from the time it had entered combat.

The 11th Armored Division had captured 76,229 German prisoners and liberated 5,012 Allied prisoners of war. In the process it had sustained 432 men killed in action, 90 who died of wounds, and 2,394 wounded in action. The 11th Armored Division was inactivated at Urfahr, Austria, on 31 August 1945.

When Hartman enlisted in the Army Reserves on 18 May 1943, little did he know that eighteen months later he would be driving a tank into combat in one of the most momentous battles of the war. Here, then, is his account of his journey to the Battle of the Bulge and beyond.

Spencer C. Tucker
Virginia Military Institute

PREFACE

I enlisted in the Army Reserves on May 18, 1943, a few days after graduating from high school with the plan to enroll in college and at least begin my higher education. Just eight weeks later, on July 22nd, I was called to active duty. From the day I entered the army until I was discharged, I made it a habit to write a letter to my parents every few days. This practice served me well through almost three years in the army, although it was not always possible when in combat.

My parents kept all of the letters I had written, which by the time of discharge numbered around 300. I edited my letters from combat days into a small volume entitled *One Thousand Fighting Miles,* which I published for family and close friends. The idea for *Tank Driver* came when a number of persons who read the earlier book suggested that I expand it using additional material from the letters.

Tank Driver is written with the expressions and slang of a teenager in the 1940s and with military language of the day. The passages are taken from my letters of that era and are phrased as written at that time.

The letters described basic training, three months in an Army Specialized Training Program (ASTP) at the University of Oregon and, when ASTP was discontinued, my experiences in the 11th Armored Division at Camp Cooke, California.

At Camp Cooke, I was assigned to the 41st Tank Battalion, where I was designated a tank driver. After intensive training, the 11th Armored Division was sent to England and on to Europe. We participated in the deadly fighting in Belgium during the Battle of the Bulge, fought through Germany and into Austria before the European war ended on May 8, 1945. I served in the Army of Occupation in Germany before being sent home for discharge on March 14, 1946.

The intent of this book is not to relate the complete history of a military campaign, although it does include details from many of our battles from Belgium to Germany to Austria. It serves to chronicle daily events in the life of a young soldier during his entire experience from the time of enlistment until discharge from the army. As I reread the letters, various incidents during my army days brought back memories of other events, a number of them humorous and a good many of them sad.

ACKNOWLEDGMENTS

As a newcomer to the process of writing a book, I must first say thanks to my wife, Jean, who has encouraged me in the task and faithfully participated in the reading and re-reading of the manuscript many times over. To our children, Jim Hartman, Tom Hartman, and Martha Hartman Schutte, go my appreciation for their support and suggestions.

At the very beginning, I was fortunate to meet Wayne Miller over the Internet. As a best-selling author, Wayne knows many of the pitfalls new writers encounter and is willing to share them with those of us who are less knowledgeable. Throughout the authoring process, he advised me in the proper methods. As we neared the time to seek a publisher, he provided the guidance to pursue that process successfully.

When it came time to develop campaign maps, Lucia Barbato of the Geography Department at Texas Tech University gave unstintingly of her time, interest, and breadth of knowledge to the project. I am very grateful to her.

Docteur Jean Lewalle of Belgium is a friend I met at an international orthopaedic surgery meeting some years ago. He and his wife, Nicole, and their friends André and Monique Burnotte and the late Françoise Neven have encouraged our visits to Belgium, opened their homes to us, and provided gracious hospitality over the past several years.

The Sherman tank that has stood on a pedestal in McAuliffe Square, Bastogne, Belgium, for over fifty years was thought to have been a tank from the 4th Armored Division because the 4th was the first army unit to reach surrounded Bastogne. After careful and detailed study, historians from the Cercle d'Histoire de Bastogne identified the tank as Barracuda of Company B, 41st Tank Battalion, 11th Armored Division. Appreciation for this effort goes to Jacques Degive, Robert Fergloute, and Roger Marquet.

To all of those who participated in this project, Jean and I say a hearty "Thanks!"

TANK DRIVER

1

The Army Beckons

In 1943, I was a high school senior in Ames, Iowa. The world
was at war and the United States was deeply involved in that war.
It was an accepted fact that every male would be called into one of
the armed services upon reaching the age of 18. Early that year, all
of the boys in my class were invited to take the A-12/V-12 examination given by the army and the navy. When those of us taking
the examination scored above a certain level, we would qualify to
be sent to a university by the armed service of our choice and
would avoid the draft.

Those preferring the navy would enlist in that branch and be
enrolled directly into the V-12 program at designated universities
across the nation. Those choosing the army were to enlist and be
assured of at least six months of university work before being
called to active duty. Once activated, the recruit would be sent for
thirteen weeks of basic training followed by enrollment in the
Army Specialized Training Program (ASTP) at a university. Several of my classmates and I received letters that we had passed, so
we hitchhiked to Des Moines, Iowa, where we went to the army recruiting station and enlisted on May 18, 1943. After a physical examination, we were sworn in as members of the Army of the
United States on inactive duty.

After graduation from high school in May, I enrolled at Iowa

State College as a premedical student. Shortly thereafter, I received a letter from the army calling me to active duty on July 22nd; this was much sooner than the six months I had been promised. *So much for the word of the army,* I thought—a thought I would have over and over again. Before leaving for the army, though, I was able to complete requirements in several courses and to receive university credit hours.

On July 22nd, I joined a number of other 18-year-olds and reported to the army recruiting station in Des Moines. From there we were driven in the back end of an army truck to Camp Dodge, the center designated to receive new troops from the State of Iowa, where we took a general IQ test and a mechanical aptitude test.

We were also given a perfunctory physical examination. This was followed by a tetanus injection, and since many of the men had never received one, the major concern during our wait in line was how each of us would react to the shot. The man in front of me, a large man of Scandinavian descent named Quam, stood bravely as the needle plunged into his arm. He promptly fainted and hit the floor, adding to our apprehension. Somehow, the rest of us received the injection without further event.

We were next given woolen army uniforms in the middle of July. Even if they were olive drab, the trousers I received were of a fine gabardine material. Everyone else had received wool flannel trousers. I became the envy of the boys in my barracks. As it turned out, the supply clerk had inadvertently reversed the sizes for my waist and leg lengths and so had given me the last pair of a rare edition of Regular Army enlisted men's trousers. It didn't matter that the waist was too tight and the legs were too long. We were told that there would be no clothing exchanges until we had reached our permanent base. I was able to get the trouser legs shortened but received no help with the tight waist until months later, at my own expense. Not only was I wearing heavy wool trousers in July; they didn't fit.

We also learned how to sign an army payroll voucher. In the process, we were all urged to sign up for a war bond each month. My pay as an army private was $65 a month, a pretty heady sum for a kid who thought he was well paid when earning 25 cents an hour for manual labor. Each war bond cost $18.75 and with earned interest it would increase to a value of $25 in ten years. The bond would be mailed to our home each month. We were told that we must list someone as the co-owner in the event that something happened to us, so I listed my father. Suddenly, I realized that they were telling me that I might not survive the war. What a blow to a teenager who expected to live forever!

We were allowed visitors at Camp Dodge, so on my first Sunday there, my parents, using some precious rationed gas (the ration was four gallons a week for ordinary citizens), came for a last visit before we were to leave for basic training. They were extremely proud of me for serving our country, yet at the same time were very concerned about where all of this was going to lead. Of course, I was feeling those very same concerns. It was a bittersweet visit.

One week following our arrival at Camp Dodge, we were marched to the train station and boarded Pullman sleeping cars for a trip to some undisclosed location. Although we had seen those fancy Pullman cars on passing trains, few of us had ever been inside one, much less ridden in one. In those days, the air-conditioning in sleeping cars was created by fans that blew air over blocks of ice under the car before it was piped inside. But the cars that were assigned to the army did not even have that system. So to try to stay cool when the train was moving, we opened the windows. However, that presented a problem. All of the locomotives were powered by steam engines that were fired by coal. The coal-burning engines constantly emitted masses of soot, which promptly blew in through the open windows. There was no way to keep clean. That was the state of travel in 1943.

The train took us to Des Moines and parked us on a rail siding near the depot. Most of us went to bed, but some of the older men left the train and went out on a bender. When they returned to the train, they were a noisy and disgusting sight. As a naïve 18-year-old, this was a real eye-opener. During the night the train pulled out, and when we awoke the next morning we were nearing Kansas City. We had a layover of several hours there, so we visited the USO (United Service Organization) Club. The USO was an organization of a concerned and unified nation staffed by volunteers that provided social opportunities for servicemen near military installations and at train stations. These clubs offered refreshments, dances, and other activities where servicemen could meet young girls serving as hostesses.

In both Des Moines and Kansas City, our train was connected

to other troop trains. From Kansas City, we headed west and south. When awakened the next morning, we were in Santa Rosa, New Mexico. I had written a letter to my parents, so when the train stopped at Alamogordo, I asked the conductor if I had time to mail it. He said that there was plenty of time, so I ran into the depot and mailed the letter. When I stepped back outside the station, I saw that the train was just beginning to move. I ran as fast as I could and jumped on. What a close shave!

Then south to El Paso, Texas, where we were combined with another troop train from the east. By then, our train was comprised of twenty Pullman cars and two dining cars. We enjoyed stops in Bisbee and Phoenix, Arizona, where Red Cross volunteers were serving homemade cookies, various cold drinks, and coffee. That was our first contact with the Red Cross and the many activities it provided for servicemen. I wrote to my mother and suggested that she and her friends should start a similar program at home. One of the women's groups that she belonged to organized a canteen at the local railroad station in cooperation with the home economics faculty from Iowa State College. They were assisted by local college girls, who had a great time meeting boys there.

We had eaten several meals in the diner and by this time had begun to understand that the waiters expected to receive a tip. They brashly passed a silver bowl to every table at each meal and made it clear that they expected some monetary thanks. None of us was familiar with the custom of leaving tips, but we were learning. However, in western Arizona, heavy rain and flooding delayed the train. We sat in the Yuma station over the dinner hour without being fed. The kitchen staff knew that one of the dining cars was to be taken off of the train there, so they refused to start cooking until they knew which car was to remain. Dinner was finally served at 10 P.M. and was so awful that when they passed the silver bowl for tips, not a single coin was put in it. The service was much better at breakfast the following morning.

When the attendant woke us up on the third morning, he told us that we were nearing Los Angeles and that our train would stay there all day. So we could leave and spend the day in town. However, the train would leave for Camp Roberts promptly at 7 P.M., and we had better be on it.

Since none of our group had been in Los Angeles before, we wandered around the city most of the morning. It was common knowledge among soldiers that the action was really in Hollywood, so several of us caught a taxi to go to the movie capital that afternoon. We found the Stage Door Canteen, a much-publicized club for servicemen that was provided and frequented by movie stars. However, it would not be open until 8 P.M., and by that time we would be on the train headed for Camp Roberts. Next, we located the corner of Hollywood and Vine Streets, which was recognized as the cross-roads of the movie industry. We also visited the Brown Derby Night Club, the Plaza Hotel, and Grauman's Chinese Theater, all spots made famous by Hollywood stars. Admission to all of these places was free, but at age 18, we could only purchase soft drinks.

In L.A., we were surprised to see women working at jobs we always considered to be man's work. They were driving large buses and taxicabs and serving as policemen, among other tasks. One woman cab driver scared us to death as she raced another cab back to the train station.

Hollywood, with the support of the movie industry and its stars, put out a tremendous effort to offer many activities and entertainment for servicemen. As our train pulled out of the station that night, we knew that we would be back.

2

Basic Training at Camp Roberts

Our train from Los Angeles took most of the night to reach Camp Roberts, California, where it pulled onto a siding that took us directly into the camp, arriving at 6 A.M. Army trucks met us and took us to the barracks of the 51st Field Artillery Battalion. The first part of the process for us was to be interviewed to see if we had any special skills that would determine where we might be assigned. I had taken typing in high school; once the interviewer learned this, he decided that I would go to the army clerical school. Those of us designated as clerks were then trucked over to the 56th Field Artillery Battalion, where all of those attending clerical school were assigned.

Slightly more than two weeks had elapsed since being called to active duty and we were settled into typical army barracks at Camp Roberts, ready to start basic training. Camp Roberts was a huge army camp constructed near the Pacific Coast halfway between Los Angeles and San Francisco. The purpose from the very beginning was to provide basic training for soldiers in both infantry and field artillery. It was a temporary military installation and was very plain and utilitarian. (Despite its "temporary" classification, it is still in use by the army today, over fifty years later.)

The parade ground where we learned to march and perform close-order drill was paved with asphalt. More often than not, however, the parade ground was covered with sand blown in by the constant winds from the Pacific Ocean.

All buildings on the base were also very plain. The barracks were two-story wooden buildings with the outside painted an olive drab. The interior walls were of a tan fiberboard material. All of the woodwork was unfinished pine. The first and second floors each contained spaces for twenty-four soldiers, twelve on each side.

The beds were simple metal frames three feet wide by six feet long on metal legs. A single layer of metal springs was attached to the frame. On the springs lay a thin mattress made of blue-and-white-striped ticking that was stuffed with cotton. When the bed was made up, it was covered with a wool olive-drab blanket pulled taut in all directions, army style, so that a "dime thrown on the bed would bounce twelve inches high." On the wall at the head of each bed was a bar to hang our uniforms on. Above this was an unpainted wooden shelf. We never knew the purpose of this shelf, as we were not allowed to place anything on it. At the foot of each bed was a wooden footlocker painted olive drab that held our underwear, socks, and personal possessions.

The barracks floors were typical three-inch tongue-and-groove unpainted pine boards that showed evidence of much wear and frequent scrubbing. At the back end of the first floor in each barracks was the latrine area. On the back wall of each latrine, there were ten washbasins lined up side by side. Along the opposite wall was a long urinal. A third wall had ten regular toilets. A door in the wall by the toilets led to the showers, where there were ten showerheads. There were no privacy separators in the entire latrine area.

Between the first-floor beds and the latrine were stairs leading to the second floor. The front of the second floor was a repeat of the beds on the first floor. Over the latrine area were four rooms for noncommissioned officers.

When we arrived at Camp Roberts, we were told that basic training had been lengthened and was now seventeen weeks instead of the thirteen weeks we had been promised when we enlisted. *So much for the word of the army.*

Our day began at 5:45 A.M., when lights were turned on in the barracks. We quickly shaved and dressed. When reveille was played over the loudspeaker, we joined in a military formation at 6:30 A.M. in the battalion marching area, where roll call was taken.

After dismissal, we went to the mess hall for breakfast. The breakfast menu could vary from ground beef in white sauce dumped on a piece of cold toast during the week to eggs and bacon or pancakes on Sunday. By 7:30 A.M., we were engaged in the training program for the day. At 11:30 A.M., we stopped for an hour and had the main meal. We resumed training from 1:00 to 5 P.M., at which time taps were played. The evening meal, which was lighter than lunch, was served at 5:30 P.M. To this day, I remember the goat stew on rice that we seemed to have every Saturday for the evening meal. It was certainly different than any meat that I was familiar with.

Most of the time, we were allowed to take care of our personal needs from supper until bedtime. During that time, I would typically go to the Service Club, where there were small desks for writing letters, a post office, a library, and a cafeteria. Any social activities would likely occur at the Service Club. We were usually exhausted at the end of the day so did not mind the lights in the barracks being turned out at 9 P.M. However, it was wise to be finished with bedtime preparations before lights went out.

For the initial five weeks we were immersed in basic training for field artillery soldiers. Some of the instruction was in classrooms (films about venereal diseases, how to care for guns, how to man an artillery piece, etc.), but a large part of it was physical. This included learning close-order drill and how to march on long hikes. Some hikes were as short as five to seven miles, but many of them were up to fifteen miles long. During this time, we attended cannoneer's school to learn the duties of the various positions required for firing the artillery cannon.

Every Tuesday there was an overnight bivouac (campout) in a wilderness area somewhere on the Camp Roberts Military Reservation. Usually we marched between five and ten miles to reach the campsite. At the end of five weeks, according to our platoon sergeant, we had marched 152 miles. During these bivouacs, we were taught the proper way to maintain public health such as how to wash our eating utensils and keep them sanitary when in the field. We also learned how and where to dig latrines so they would not drain into other areas that would create a public health hazard. We were taught

Basic training: Soldier Ted Hartman, age 18, at Camp Roberts, California.

how to dig foxholes that would protect us from direct gunfire or tanks. One vital instruction was how to walk guard duty.

During basic training, we were taught the care and firing of various weapons, carbines, submachine guns, bazookas, and so forth. The weapon used by the field artillery that was most often assigned to us was the carbine. Because of the possibility that the enemy would use poison gases, we were taught the proper use of gas masks and how to recognize different gases upon smell. We were even taken through drills in which token amounts of the various gases were sprayed in the air. We crawled through infiltration courses with explosions occurring near us while live bullets were being fired over our heads to teach us to keep a low profile. We were graded severely on how well we had performed in all of these exercises, which seem to have been designed with one practical purpose in mind—our safety in battle.

After several days of classes and movies on driver's education during basic field artillery training, we went out on practical driving experiences. We drove a four-wheel-drive truck up and down several steep hills. While I was driving down one particularly steep downhill grade in low gear, the gearshift popped out of four-wheel drive. We fairly flew down that hill while I tried to keep the rear end from swinging around. The officer with us was certain I had not handled the gear properly until he drove the course and the same thing happened. I felt vindicated when he admitted that we had a defective truck. We drove several different types of vehicles from the jeep up to the 4 × 4 truck. After our classes and experiences, I received an army driver's license for those vehicles.

Every Saturday morning there was an official inspection of the barracks. This included examination of our uniforms, the firearm assigned to each of us, and whatever else the inspecting officer decided to look at that morning. Preparing our barracks for inspection took all of Friday evening. We had to sweep the floors first and then, on our hands and knees, scrub those floors with bristle brushes and army-issue (lye) soap and water. When finished, the floor had been "GIed," in army language. The latrine had to be spotless. We used Bon Ami cake soap to clean the sinks, toilets, and urinal. We were also required to polish the exposed copper pipes with Bon Ami.

When the officer came into the barracks for inspection, we were required to stand at attention at the foot of our bed. It was rare that we didn't receive a demerit on some item to which we had given special attention. There was no way to win, nor was there any way to identify what particular thing would be the target at the next inspection. All of this was part of learning discipline, we were told. And through all of these new activities, no one was killed or even injured from the actions of inexperienced soldiers.

An example of a typical exercise in learning discipline was the time I was given a special detail to perform at the same time that we were to eat supper. I was told to go and water the lawn of the colonel's house for an hour and a half. By doing that, I missed the meal, of course.

Abruptly, it seemed, basic training ended and we were assigned to clerical training for the next twelve weeks. Except for close-order drill exercises, weekly bivouacs on Tuesday nights, and the ever-present Saturday morning inspections, we spent our days in classrooms learning army forms, army regulations, army methods for records and, of course, improving our typing skills. Clerical training was pretty intense but taught us a good sense of how the army functions. It was a thorough education which served us well in later times.

While we were there, some well-known entertainers, including Blackstone the Magician, Judy Garland, and Red Skelton came to Camp Roberts and presented stage shows. The movie *See Here, Private Hargrove* was also being filmed on location, so one evening the actors presented a stage show of some of the episodes for us.

In the 1940s, making a long-distance telephone call was a major event. The process of making the call was very labor intensive, as there was almost no automation. When the operator in the originating city answered the ring, she would ask for the destination city and telephone number. A connection would be made to the next city on the route designated for the call. That operator would connect the call to the telephone exchange of the next city on the route. This action would be repeated until the call reached the destination exchange. The operator at the final exchange would connect the call to the receiving telephone. All the while, the operator at the originating exchange would remain on the line until the destination party answered the phone. Because of the complexity and cost of such calls, it was rare to receive a long-distance call unless there was a major emergency. (There were no touch-tone telephones and no area codes in that era.)

I did call home one time from Camp Roberts. I went to the Service Club, where there was an operator, and gave her the telephone number and location I wished to call. She checked the lines from Camp Roberts to Ames, Iowa, and informed me that there would be a four-hour delay. This call was routed through Omaha, and other calls placed before it had priority.

In early November, we were sent out to the Hunter Liggett Military Reservation, adjacent to Camp Roberts, for two weeks to acquire additional experiences. This gave us a much broader and deeper understanding of what battle might be like. During that time, we repeatedly dug foxholes and latrines, served on KP (kitchen police), and walked guard duty nightly, all the while trying to stay warm in early winter weather. While we were there, I was called out and sent back into Camp Roberts to be interviewed by a board of officers who were deciding which soldiers would be sent to an Army Specialized Training Program (ASTP).

In the waning days of clerical training at Camp Roberts, I learned that I would be assigned to the ASTP at the University of Oregon in Eugene. This location was fortunate for me, as the University of Oregon was a medium-sized classical liberal arts university and Eugene was a typical college town, similar to Ames, Iowa, where I was raised.

As things began to wind down at Camp Roberts, on our last afternoon, the two of us who were to be sent to the University of Oregon were called to the supply room and told to turn in all of our field equipment. These were the items that we used when out camping, such as our web belt (a heavy cotton belt with metal grommets in it to attach our water canteen, a weapon holster, etc.). They also took our plastic helmet liner (the steel helmet was only issued to soldiers when going overseas), our extra blankets, and our ugly heavy olive-drab overcoat. In exchange, we were issued three extra pairs of woolen socks, another tan cotton uniform, and a very nice tan mackinaw (a three-quarter-length coat for use in winter weather). I then packed my duffel bag with everything except what I would need for the last night.

Having the night off, I went to see Bruce Ross, a close high school friend who had been in infantry basic training also at Camp Roberts. Six of us who were friends in high school had been sent there at about the same time. We had been able to get together some, especially on weekends, and had bolstered each other's morale. It was a very hard parting, as Bruce was the last one of our group remaining at Camp Roberts.

The following day, just as we were getting ready to leave, the battery commander came to our barracks and called all of us together. He said that someone had taken $15 from Heath, one of the soldiers in our barracks. In 1943, that was a very significant sum of money. Heath had hidden the money in a carefully concealed place that only a neighbor might have observed. This was early December, and it was money that Heath planned to use to purchase Christmas gifts for his wife and new baby.

Just as the battery commander was talking to us about this, the military police arrived and brought the case to a conclusion. They had used fingerprints to identify one of the soldiers in our barracks as the guilty person. He was a soldier who had gone through basic training and clerical training with us. He was also identified as the person involved in other episodes of stealing that had been reported in our barracks. The guilty soldier would receive a trial by court-martial (a military court) for the offense. This type of activity was a definite risk where a large number of persons lived together so closely and so openly. With the case solved, all of us with travel orders were dismissed to go our separate ways.

We carried our duffel bags about three blocks to the adjutant general's office, where we were checked out, loaded on army trucks, and taken to the nearby Paso Robles train station to board a train for Oakland.

When we arrived at the train station, we found fifteen friends waiting there who had been accepted for ASTP upon completion of basic training. However, just prior to shipment, they were notified by the army that they would not be sent to ASTP. Instead, they were being sent to Camp Hale, Colorado, where they were assigned to a mule-pack artillery battery and would be trained for winter warfare in the mountains. Seeing those boys to whom ASTP had been promised but who were instead being sent to a combat unit was sobering. What did the future hold for us? *So much for the word of the army.*

3

ASTP at the University of Oregon

The train we boarded in Paso Robles was the regularly scheduled train that ran from Los Angeles to Oakland. When we reached Oakland, we swung our duffel bags (which held all of our earthly possessions) onto our backs, climbed off the train, and set out to find the railroad car that we were to board for the next segment of our trip. When we asked for directions, we were directed out to the freight yard.

After walking for what seemed like several miles, we found our car, a strange-looking thing that reminded us of a small freight car. It turned out to be the latest in troop transport, called a troop sleeper. Six men rode in facing seats in each compartment by day and then, at night, converted it into three stacked bunks on each side that were crosswise to the car. The head of the bed was at the windows on one side while the feet rested toward the aisle which ran by the windows on the opposite side of the car. Each car contained six similar compartments. We were told that the troop sleeper was smaller, lighter, and held more men (thirty-six) than a typical Pullman car. The bunks were quite comfortable, long enough, wide enough, and definitely better than a short, cramped Pullman bed.

When we awoke the next morning, we were passing through Weed, a major producer of forest products in northern California. As the train moved north into Oregon, we saw around us beautiful timbered country with numerous small logging settlements along the railroad. We passed Klamath Lake, Crescent Lake, and many smaller lakes that were used as sawmill ponds (logs were stored in these ponds until they were ready to be sawed into lumber). My father was a forester, so I was familiar with this phase of wood utilization and enjoyed seeing these beautiful forested areas. The train stopped at a mountain summit for the steam engine to take on water, so several of us jumped off the train and had a brief snowball fight. We had not seen snow for many months. Late that afternoon we reached our destination, Eugene. Even in December, the landscape was lush and green, a major contrast to arid Camp Roberts.

At the train station we were met by soldiers who drove us out to the University of Oregon in army trucks. It was a beautiful campus with lovely trees and broad expanses of green, green grass. At the dormitory we were assigned to temporary rooms and then sent to the dining hall for dinner. In sharp contrast to army food, the meals here were delicious. We learned that the cooks and waitresses were all women from Eugene who were regular employees of the university.

The ASTP soldiers at Oregon who had just completed a quarter's study were home on a week's furlough, so we would not start classes until they returned. One afternoon, a friend and I walked to town to look for a chain for my dog tags. The dog tag was a small metal plaque that was issued on a tape to wear around our neck. It identified us by name, serial number, and religion in the event we were killed in battle. I found a sterling silver chain that I really liked and told the store owner I wished to purchase it. He promptly gave it to me, *gave* it to me. What a surprise!

Following that, we stopped at an ice cream shop for a sundae. A man came in, sat down beside us at the counter and had a cup of coffee. He was very friendly, and we talked until he finished his coffee and left. When we started to pay our bill, we were told that it had already been paid by the man who had been sitting next to us. We had not even been able to thank him. This sort of treatment was new to us, and we liked it.

On the third day, we were given a test to identify the level of our competence in mathematics, and then were assigned to our permanent rooms. My room was on the ground floor of the dormitory, which I shared with a soldier named McGrath. There was a washbasin and a toilet in a recess off the room. The shower was next door. This was quite a contrast to the barracks at Camp Roberts.

Most soldiers wore a patch on the upper left sleeve of their uniform that identified the organization to which they belonged. Because soldiers in basic training were not yet assigned to a permanent unit, they did not wear a patch. When we signed in at the University of Oregon, we were given patches to sew on our uniforms for the first time.

The ASTP patch was square with rounded corners. The background was yellow with a blue lamp of knowledge in the center. Through it was a sword in contrasting blue and yellow. When sewed on the sleeve, the patch was rotated forty-five degrees so that the lamp of knowledge sat upright. Though we were not the most accomplished at sewing, we all busily sewed the patches on our uniforms and proudly wore them.

If a family had a member on active duty in the armed services during World War II, it was common for that family to display a service flag in a prominent window to indicate their participation in the war. In the center of the red-bordered white flag was a blue star (or stars), representing each family member serving his country. If a member of the family had been killed, the blue star was replaced with a gold one.

"Take down that service flag, your son's in ASTP." That's the way *Yank Magazine* referred to the Army Specialized Training Program in an article written in December 1943. *Yank* then qualified the statement by saying that ASTP was halfway "GI" while the other half was hard work.

On the first Sunday in Eugene, I arose early, ate breakfast, and walked downtown to church, a beautiful, old colonial-style building. Coming home, I passed several fraternity and sorority houses. It was nice to know where the sorority houses were for future reference. They were mostly along the Mill Race, an old creek that flowed out of a sawmill pond at the south end of the university campus. The meal this noon was extra nice—baked chicken, dressing, mashed potatoes, asparagus, milk, and ice cream. Those ladies really worked hard to prepare our meals.

Christmas was coming. I received numerous Christmas cards,

letters, and a number of boxes from my parents, relatives, and friends. Many of the boxes contained homemade cookies and candies, all made with scarce rationed sugar.

In a letter to my folks, I commented that it looked as though Christmas would be different this year with two sons and a son-in-law in the army, but that there would always be another Christmas next year and perhaps we would be together then. Little did I know.

Christmas morning I went to church and had a visit with some other soldiers who were in the Army Air Corps pre-meteorology program at the University of Oregon (the Air Corps was a branch of the army during World War II). These soldiers had enlisted in the Air Corps specifically to be sent for meteorology training and had just been informed that their program would be discontinued the following May. The Air Corps explained that they had over-estimated their needs. *So much for the word of the army.*

Mrs. Turnipseed, who was in charge of the dormitory and the dining hall, looked out for all of "her boys." At Christmas time, she placed bowls of fresh fruit and nuts in the lobby of our dormitory. She planned a beautiful Christmas dinner with turkey and all of the trimmings. We felt sorry for the women who had to work on Christmas Day, but we were told that none of them had to work because of need; it was their way to help the war effort. This was not an uncommon feeling among people throughout the country.

It was a few days after Christmas that I received word that Ralph Paulson, a friend and neighbor of many years, had been killed in a marine battle in the Pacific. It left a really dull feeling in the pit of my stomach. It was so close to home, just barely outside of our family. My brother, George, was especially close to Ralph. The news really hit him hard. It was so sad for Ralph's mother, as she had lived a very hard life and had been such a strong person through it all. To lose a son like this was devastating. Ralph's brothers, the twins, flying in the Air Corps, were in a dangerous arm of the service but did not suffer injury during the war.

Our instructors were regular university professors. Some of them, however, had been asked to teach subjects out of their area of expertise. It was interesting, though, that our math professor, who had taught journalism before the war, was actually quite a good mathematics teacher. With many members of the faculty away on war assignment, it was difficult for universities to cover some of the subjects required by the army.

Classes began in early January and were going okay. Most of us thought that our performance was acceptable. So I was quite surprised to receive a "valentine" at midterm in chemistry, as we had only had one test in the course and the teacher told me I had gotten a C on it. A "valentine" at the University of Oregon was a notice that you had received a D or a D-minus in some course. Chemistry turned out to be a real problem for me, as it was quite different from the course that I had taken at Iowa State. Partway through the semester we were given tests to determine whether or not we would be allowed to continue in ASTP. My scores were satisfactory in all of the subjects except chemistry, in which I received a C. I kept working at it and gradually began to grasp the subject.

Because I had to take so many notes in class, the valve and bladder on my Eversharp pen broke. Pens in that era had bladders that needed to be filled with liquid ink from a bottle; there were no ballpoint pens. I sent the pen to its manufacturer in Chicago to get it repaired and was surprised to have it repaired and returned at no cost. The invoice stated that they did not charge servicemen. There were some benefits.

We tried to maintain an academic record, but we also recognized that we were at a civilian university and that there were also girls on the campus. We were off duty at 3 P.M. one Saturday afternoon, so Brig Young and I cleaned up and after supper went to the Nickel Hop. The idea was for the boys to go to any sorority house they wished and pay a nickel for three dances with a girl of his choice. There was no student union building on the University of Oregon campus, so the proceeds were to go toward construction of one. We went to several of the sorority houses and danced. Then Brig felt the necessity to go back to a house where he had been smitten with one of the girls. The following night he was out with the same girl again. As you can tell, we thought we were quite the campus Casanovas. With most of the male students gone to war, we weren't faced with lots of competition.

Another very pleasant diversion for me in Eugene was meeting Helen and Ed Bailey. Ed was very active as an advisor to my fraternity. They had frequent gatherings for us at their home. Ed and Helen had lost their only child, a son, in a tragic swimming accident when he was a senior in high school. They craved the companionship of young people. Helen was an excellent cook and always had delicious food ready for us to eat. They were such lovely people. I was able to visit them after the war and to enjoy continued contact until their deaths.

In a letter to my parents in late January, I said, "I hung onto the last ten dollar bill I had until last evening when I had to get a haircut for $1.00." This shows the value of a dollar at that time and why we were so careful about spending money.

My grades continued to be A's and B's, so from an academic standpoint, I was doing fine. But somehow there seemed to be a growing sense that the ASTP program was losing favor and might not be as stable as we hoped. We were given tests that were standardized throughout all of the ASTP units, but found many of the questions were on subjects in which we had received no instruction. There just seemed to be increasing confusion about the entire program. But from my past experience, it did not seem inconsistent with the way the army did things.

Although nothing definite was forthcoming, we continued to hear rumors about closure of the ASTP program nationally. At one point we even received a copy of an announcement from the War Department which stated that the ASTP program was not in the process of liquidation, as some news sources had claimed. However, quotas would be changed from time to time, according to needs. That sounded suspicious to us.

Two months after arriving at the University of Oregon, we were finally told that most of the ASTP programs would be closed. When they heard this, many of the boys quit studying and decided to have a good time. The study halls became noisy. Those of us who continued to study bore the brunt of many jokes and comments. There was no definite information, so it was possible that we might still be in school the next semester. It was a difficult time, but I felt strongly that I needed to make the most of the situation.

Finally, an announcement was made that all ASTP programs were to be closed except for medicine and foreign languages and that most of the soldiers in ASTP would be sent to army ground units to be trained for battle. And that is exactly what happened. The full story is told in the Army Service Forces Memorandum of

February 21, 1944. Many of the combat soldiers injured or killed in action from late 1944 until the end of the European war in May 1945 were bright young men who had enlisted in the army with the promise of being sent to the Army Specialized Training Program. *So much for the word of the army.*

When I enlisted, I had a choice of going into the army or into a naval air corps program which would have sent me to a university followed by flight training. My father, who had served in the army in World War I, had suggested that I go the army route. His concern arose from the fact that four of his former students had been in the naval air corps in the Pacific, were shot down, and were never heard from again. Because of the encouragement he had given me, he felt bad when the ASTP program was discontinued.

I wrote to my parents at that time and said, "Yes, the Naval Air Corps university program followed by flight training was a good deal in many ways. But if you get shot down in the middle of the Pacific, what do you have below you to parachute onto?" I reassured him that it was my decision to believe the promises of the army and that I would make the most of what came. I still have that conviction to this day despite some of the events described in this book.

At the taps ceremony the last afternoon, our commandant, Major Averill, confirmed that everyone in the ASTP unit at the University of Oregon was being sent to the 11th Armored Division, which was stationed at Camp Cooke, California.

On the last evening in Eugene, I went over to tell the Baileys goodbye. It did all of us good to just spend a little quiet time together. When I got home, an instinct told me to check my bed. When I pulled the covers back, I found my bed filled with army soap, shaving cream, sand, and other sundry things. Three of the boys had "fixed" almost everyone's bed. We found out who the culprits were, so during the night, after all of them were asleep, several of us who had been victims found buckets in the housekeeping closet and managed to pour buckets of frigid water on the perpetrators. A truce the following morning stopped further activities of that nature.

The final day at Oregon, we spent most of the morning checking in equipment that had been assigned to us, followed by room inspection. After that we were free until time to march from the Oregon campus down to the train station. So Brig Young and I

ARMY SERVICE FORCES
ASTU 3920

UNIV OF ORE
EUGENE, ORE
21 FEB 44

MEMORANDUM: All Trainees

The following radiogram received from the Secretary of War is repeated for your information:

"You were assigned to the Army Specialized Training Program because it was felt that the courses of instruction scheduled would materially increase your value to the Military Service. You have been working under high pressure to master as quickly as possibly those essentials of college training of greatest importance to your development as a soldier.

"The time has now come for the majority of you to be assigned to other active duty. To break the enemies defenses and force their unconditional surrender, it is necessary to hit them with the full weight of America's manpower. Because of this imperative military necessity most of you will soon be ordered to field service before completion of your normal course.

"The Army Specialized Training Program will be reduced prior to 1 April 1944 to 35,000 trainees which will include 5,000 pre-induction students and advanced medical, dental, and engineering groups, the US Military Academy preparatory course and certain language groups. Most of you released from the ASTP will be assigned to the Army Ground Forces for duty with divisions and other units. Your intelligence, training, and high qualities of leadership are expected to raise the combat efficiency of those units.

"The thousands of ASTP trainees who have already been assigned to field service have set high standards for you to follow."

By order of the Secretary of War:

W. S. AVERILL
Major, Infantry
Commandant

This memo was received by all ASTP soldiers at the University of Oregon.

went canoeing on the Mill Race. Neither of us knew much about canoeing, so that added to the fun of it.

Late that afternoon, we assembled, were given our train car assignments, and then marched en masse down to the train station. The streets were lined with local people there to bid us farewell. Many of our officers and noncommissioned officers were at the station to see us off. And, Mrs. Turnipseed, bless her heart, was there with some of the women from the dining room to wave goodbye.

We boarded the train. As it began to move, we all realized that this was the end of a most pleasant, never to be repeated, experience in the army. *Camp Cooke, for better or worse, here we come.*

4

Camp Cooke

The special troop train was full, carrying 500 soldiers who had been in the Army Specialized Training Program at the University of Oregon. The 11th Armored Division, to which all of us were assigned, had sent officers, noncommissioned officers, and mess sergeants (cooks) to be in charge of our entire group. The mess sergeants set up kitchens in two baggage cars and fed us our meals en route. We even had a doctor on board who conducted daily sick call.

Our destination was Camp Cooke, California, an armored force base located near the Pacific Ocean, a little more than 100 miles north of Los Angeles. The route of travel was the reverse of the one we had taken to Eugene four months earlier. Having boarded the train in the early evening, we slept through southern Oregon and northern California, so missed the timber country. We did see Alcatraz and the Golden Gate Bridge as we came through the Bay Area. There were numerous shipyards and many ships docked at wharves.

On the train, army indecision reigned. The night we were to reach Camp Cooke, we had been instructed to go to bed by 10 P.M. Then we were awakened at midnight and told to get up and get dressed, as we were approaching the camp. After another hour and a half of catnaps, we finally arrived. As everyone climbed off the train we were greeted by a group of officers and noncommissioned officers from the 11th Armored Division.

The greeting party caught our attention by yelling through a loud-speaker. A lieutenant at the microphone was trying to be funny by telling jokes at 2 A.M. When we weren't responsive, he began making nasty remarks about college kids and ASTP. It was all downhill from there. We were loaded onto trucks that took us to some barracks, where we showered, had a physical examination, and were given a snack.

Then we went to a gymnasium, where we milled about for four hours while some sort of classification process went on. At 6:30 A.M. they began to read off names and assignments. I anxiously sweated through name calls giving assignments to several battalions of armored engineers, ordnance, armored infantry, signal corps, and cavalry reconnaissance before they began to call the tank battalions. There seemed to be no system to the classifications, as air corps boys went to medics, medics went to infantry, artillery went to ordnance, and so forth. Very few of our friends were placed in the same units. My friend Shors and I were sent to the same tank battalion. Geiger went to a different tank battalion. At least Brig Young, who had trained as a medic, was reassigned to the medics.

The 11th Armored Division was a mixture of medium and light tanks that had participated in Louisiana maneuvers around DeRidder, the town where I was born. During my physical examination the night we arrived at Camp Cooke, the examining doctor commented on the fact that half of the uvula of my soft palate was missing. I told him that it had been inadvertently cut off while a doctor was performing a tonsillectomy. He asked where it had been done. I replied that it was in DeRidder, Louisiana.

His rejoinder was, "Looks like something that would happen in DeRidder." It was rare for servicemen to develop a fondness for the communities near their base.

All of us newcomers were temporarily attached to Company D, a light tank company. It appeared to us that a tank company consisted of two groups. One group was the men in combat tank crews while the other group was the men who would provide services that would support the activity of the combat tank crews. The latter group included the mechanics, cooks, and supply personnel, who provided all types of supplies with the exception of food. The company commander was the highest-ranking officer in the company

Cutaway of Sherman Medium Tank. Artwork by Peter Sarson from New Vanguard 3. Osprey Publishing Ltd.

and gave direction to the first sergeant and the company clerk for administration of the company. He was also responsible for all training and combat activities of the company. After several days, the new men were assigned to their permanent company within the battalion. I was placed in Company B, a medium tank company that was still driving the Sherman tanks it had received when the division was activated at Camp Polk, Louisiana, two years earlier.

There were two types of Sherman tanks in our company. One had a cast-iron hull and was powered by an air-cooled engine that had been developed for aircraft. In the other, the hull was made of two-and-one-half-inch-thick steel plates welded together. This type used a water-cooled 600 horsepower Ford engine. The latter was the preferred one. The same cast-iron turret was used in both tanks.

Our early impression was that the 11th Armored Division was a rough outfit. A number of the men in B Company spoke of escapades when they had gone AWOL (absent without leave) and had been court-martialed for the offense. When soldiers from the 11th went on pass, they were required to take with them an R & L Kit (a prophylaxis kit to be used for the prevention of venereal diseases). I never knew what the letters R and L stood for. This gives an idea of the main activity occurring on pass.

Many of the original men had been transferred out of the division to make positions for those of us from ASTP. The commanding officer of Company B, Captain Robert L. Ameno, interviewed the twenty-five new men individually and left us with a good overall impression. He told us that he would be making assignments after we had a couple of months of training, when he would have a better idea of our capabilities.

We were immediately immersed in classes and practical experiences to teach us the basics of how to function in an armored unit. We learned about each position in the tank. In addition, we learned the detailed duties of the position to which we were assigned. My first assignment was as an assistant driver. Although most of us were inexperienced, we were given lessons and training so that we could become proficient at driving a tank and firing the turret weapons. The assistant driver had a .30-caliber machine gun as his tank weapon. In addition, in combat, each member of a tank crew carried a submachine gun strapped over his shoulder for personal protection.

The Sherman tank had positions for the driver and the assistant driver at the lower front of the cast-iron or welded steel hull. Each of these positions had a hatch for entrance and exit. The round turret sat on the hull, to which it was attached by heavy metal gears. The turret had positions for three men—the tank commander, the gunner, and the assistant gunner. There were two hatches in the turret, one over the assistant gunner and one for the tank commander. The entire crew was connected by an intercom system. All members of the tank crew wore earphones and had microphones so that they could talk between themselves. Any communication to the tank by shortwave radio could be heard by every member of the crew. However, only the tank commander could talk over the radio to the other tanks.

From his position in the turret hatch, the tank commander was the eyes and ears for the crew of five, so he was required to keep his head out of the hatch at all times. In addition to coordinating the various activities, he gave instructions to the driver regarding speed and direction of travel. He guided the gunner to a target, estimated the distance of the target, and ordered the type of projectile to be fired. While he was directing these activities, he was also receiving instructions on the radio from the platoon lieutenant and/or platoon sergeant for his ongoing participation in combat. This all required major coordination during battle.

A 75mm gun was located in the center of the turret facing forward. The breech into which ammunition was loaded was at the rear end of the gun inside the turret. A .30-caliber machine gun sat immediately to the right of the 75mm gun. The gunner was placed to the right of this machine gun at the gun sight. From there he controlled the sighting and firing of both the 75mm gun and the .30-caliber machine gun following directions given by the tank commander. The assistant gunner sat to the left of the 75mm gun and loaded ammunition into it and the machine gun as needed.

The guns were mounted on a gyrostabilizer unit that floated the guns and kept them aimed at the sighted target even when the tank was moving across uneven or irregular ground. This allowed our tanks to fire either gun with accuracy while on the move, something the Germans could not do. In order to be accurate, the Germans had to stop their tank to fire the large guns. Also, the turret on most German tanks had to be rotated by a hand crank, whereas our gunner could rotate the turret 360 degrees with an electrical control switch.

In an early letter written to my parents, I asked, "Can you imagine me as a tanker? I always thought that Son [my brother] would be more the type of person to be in a combat outfit because he is so well coordinated. However, I am sure that I can take anything that they throw at me."

The letter continued, "Right now I am at the Service Club catching up on correspondence. All of the older soldiers in the company tell us to clear out of the barracks as soon as you are off duty and don't come back until bedtime or you will be chosen for some sort of extra duty. This was good sound advice that we learned to respect and follow."

The 11th Armored Division had many little quirks we learned to accept. We were required to wear only army-issued shoes when on base. Civilian shoes were forbidden even if we were off duty but on base. Civilian shoes could be worn only when we were off base and on furlough. The wearing of a garrison cap (cap with a bill) was not allowed. The cloth overseas cap was the only head cover permitted. Soldiers in most army branches wore their cloth caps tipped to the right. Not so with the armored soldier, who wore his cap (often with the taller Fort Knox peaks at the front and back) tipped at a rakish angle to the left. The army-issue cloth cap had a peak at the front and back which was created by the head fitting into the flat envelope-shaped hat. Fort Knox peaks were an accentuation of this peak at the front and back, created by a deeper envelope. Fort Knox was the official home base of all armored activity in the army and was the original site where the high-peaked cap was worn.

Two weeks after we arrived at Camp Cooke, we were told that we would be required to have the 11th Armored Division patch sewn on the sleeves of all our uniforms by the following Saturday, which was three days later. These patches were usually available from the supply sergeant free of charge, but he had none. An order was an order, and it did not matter that there were no patches available on the entire base. So we scurried around and arranged for some of the men who were going to town on pass to buy patches for us at the local army store. These privately owned stores were in all towns near army bases and usually carried all sorts of supplies in addition to army goods. The trouble was that the patches cost 25 cents each. With ten items requiring patches, that meant we had to spend $2.50. What a rip-off.

After four weeks of basic armored training, we were tested in driving skills, principles of reconnaissance, guard duty, and poison gases. We had to identify the poison gases by smell. It wasn't hard. Some of the lewisite spray hit my face, though, and made tiny little stinging blisters. We passed all of the tests in good order, so we began to have field exercises in which we were taught general combat tactics.

As we gained a better understanding of ways to manage ourselves in combat, we began to engage in tactical exercises using the tanks. Our old tanks were filthy inside because of their previous use in desert training. Each of us was assigned used equipment that all tankers were required to have, including goggles, cloth helmets, and gas masks. The gas masks had also been used in desert training and were really filthy and crusted on the inside.

The motor park where the tanks and other vehicles were kept was across a perimeter road from the barracks area. We would march there and back at least twice each day. As an assistant driver, I had to learn to drive the tank so I could relieve the driver as needed. There was a hatch door overhead for direct entry and exit. When we finished field exercises, we would come back into the motor park and perform the necessary maintenance. As we helped maintain the tanks, we began to learn more about them and how they worked. After we became more experienced, we were allowed to drive the tanks back to the motor park from the field.

Even though we ASTP types were the youngest and least experienced men in the company, we were gradually gaining acceptance. One of the officers took us out for driving lessons to a spot about one-and-one-half miles west of camp and there it was, the Pacific Ocean. Now we understood why we battled incessant winds and blowing sand. The driving lessons were catching our interest, even though we did them in tanks that were dusty and dirty. They were really powerful old buggies that took two gallons of gas to go one mile. Because they were so old, they also broke down constantly. It kept the mechanics extremely busy.

Driving a tank did not turn out to be as simple as driving a four-wheeled vehicle. It took many lessons before I was able to coordinate gear shifting in a vehicle which weighed thirty-three tons. The gears didn't mesh smoothly, so shifting gears required double-clutching and a lot of beef. Our tank was powered by a Continental radial air-cooled engine which had been developed for aircraft but had been placed in many tanks when other engines were not available. Potential for stalling was ever present if the required number of revolutions per minute was not maintained. While concentrating on that, one had to keep control of the steering levers. The driver steered the tank by pulling a right or a left lever or, if braking, by pulling both levers simultaneously. It simply took experience at the controls to develop the coordination required.

Not until some weeks later was I given my first opportunity to drive the tank during a mock battle where we took an "enemy airfield." It was a major triumph and was, I believe, the beginning of my acceptance as part of the team. I didn't goof up, so that was a major accomplishment. After getting to know the boys better, I realized that they were a good group. There was a large contingent from the East Coast, but there was also a good spread from across the country.

In a letter to my parents, I described some of my buddies who also slept on the second floor of the barracks. Those descriptions are as follows:

> Leonard Montkowski is a private, is hard working and a good kid, but has never been willing to swallow some of the stuff necessary to get a promotion. I enjoy him.
>
> Pat Needham is an Irishman, about twenty-six years old. He has had three years of college and is a devout Roman Catholic, attends mass regularly. He was just promoted to private first class and is very disgusted with that because he considers it barely more than a private. He is bright and very interesting.
>
> Patrick McCue was in ASTP at the University of California and has had two years of college. His home is in San Jose. He is getting married soon to his college girlfriend. Very nice and likable. Humorous without intending to be.
>
> Thomas Sumners (nicknamed Paducah) is from Kentucky. There are no secrets from Paducah. He watches and asks and needs to know everything. He is interesting. We go to chapel together.
>
> John O'Loughlin from Utah was also in ASTP at University of California. A good boy.
>
> Bill Zaher is a sergeant tank commander from Chicago. Has a fine sense of humor and is well coordinated. Reads good literature.
>
> John Myers is a chubby sergeant and tank commander from Ohio. His father is a Methodist minister in Steubenville. He is very likable and has a good sense of humor.
>
> All in all, this is a very interesting group.

Several weeks after arriving at Camp Cooke, a one-time event occurred. We had a weekend visit by 120 Junior Hostesses from Los Angeles who came to visit our battalion. They stayed in the barracks next to ours, but there had been a transformation. All of a sudden we noticed curtains and other nice touches not usually seen in army barracks. We had a dance at the Service Club Saturday night and took them to chapel on Sunday morning followed by rides in jeeps and tanks. Sunday afternoon they departed and we returned to normalcy. They were a nice sociable group, even if, as I wrote to my parents, they were not all "ravishing beauties."

By early May, we had completed training in firing carbines, submachine guns, .30-caliber machine guns, and .50-caliber machine guns. The latter was located on top of the turret and was used to fire at enemy aircraft. This completed instructions required by the Army Ground Forces before we were qualified for overseas assignment.

Thinking that I would go to medical school after getting out of the army and that working in the medical corps would be good experience, I visited our battalion medical officer to discuss the possibility of becoming a medic. He told me he had never been able to get the Company B commander, Captain Robert L. Ameno, to agree to transfer a man to the medics, but he would try. So he put in a request to have me transferred, only to have the request denied. Captain Ameno then called me into his office and told me that he did not approve the transfer. He told me that as a medical corpsman, I would be out in the middle of the battlefield without a weapon to protect myself. He thought such an experience would be of no help to a future doctor. I respected his opinion and dropped the matter. After going into battle and seeing our medics riding in open jeeps out in the battlefield without weapons, I shall forever be grateful to Captain Ameno for his wise counsel and help.

As our education advanced, we acquired more and more field experiences. We went on a road march in the tank to learn how to keep up the pace with eighteen tanks moving at the same speed and arriving at the target area at the same time. From a beginner's standpoint, it was actually fun. I was still in the assistant driver's seat and became acutely aware that the tank engine was drawing air through vents in the front of the hull. I quickly learned that tanks were cold when it was cold outside and brutally hot when the weather was hot. The country where we bivouacked on that outing was very pretty even though semiarid and covered with scrub oak. It was away from the Pacific Ocean, so it was much warmer than it was at our barracks. Each of us had to walk a two-hour guard

Home on furlough in Ames, Iowa, May 1944, from Camp Cooke, California, Ted Hartman visits with parents and sister.

shift around our individual tank, a practice strictly adhered to on maneuvers and in combat.

I was in line to get a ten-day furlough to visit home, so I needed to buy a nice pair of shoes that I could wear off post. I was given a ration coupon which allowed me to purchase one pair of shoes. I went to the Officers Post Exchange and found a beautiful pair made of very fine soft brown leather. They cost $7.45, more than I had hoped, but I was able to sell my old pair of brown shoes for $4.00. I figured that I could get at least $3.45 use out of the new shoes. This gives an idea of the value of the dollar in 1944.

I received a ten-day furlough in the latter part of May 1944. An ordinary soldier could only afford to travel by coach on the train. I boarded the train in Santa Maria and went to Los Angeles. The Union Pacific Railroad did not accept seat reservations on most trains, and when I boarded the train in Los Angeles, all of the seats were taken. So on the overnight trip from Los Angeles to Denver, I had to choose between standing in the aisle or sitting on the armrest of an aisle seat. I chose to sit. Many of the passengers left the train at Denver, so I was able to get a seat for the remainder of the trip to Ames, Iowa, my destination. Most of the time on furlough was spent with family, as all of my male friends were away in the service. My sister was home on vacation from Washington, D.C., where she worked as a cryptographer for the army, coding and decoding secret messages. Using some rationed gas, we drove ninety miles to visit an aunt and her family.

At the end of the furlough, I boarded a Union Pacific train car in Ames that was a real puddle jumper. However, at Omaha, I was able to get a reclining seat in a nice coach. While we were at the depot in Denver, someone took my suitcase to the men's lounge and rummaged through it. It mysteriously reappeared on the rack over my head with nothing missing. The connection in Los Angeles to the Southern Pacific train for Santa Maria was close, and I had to rush to get a seat. As soon as the train pulled out of the station, I went to the diner and enjoyed a very nice dinner for 75 cents.

When I arrived back at Camp Cooke, I found that a number of men had been transferred to the infantry, including our first sergeant. My platoon sergeant, Lenwood Ammons, was named first sergeant. That pleased us, as we had great respect for Sergeant Ammons. Also, I found that I had been promoted to private first class. As mentioned earlier, being promoted to private first class (PFC) wasn't much of an honor. In a letter home, I told my parents of the appointment and that I wasn't thrilled about it and did not want them publicizing it. The local newspaper always published any news about men from Ames who were in the service, and I knew my folks would inform the paper. Though I did not want the appointment, I feared that if I refused it, I would have a hard time ever getting a promotion higher than that, so I kept quiet.

After I returned to Camp Cooke from furlough, the "old man," a classic army term used to refer to the commanding officer, called me in and asked me whether I preferred to be a gunner or a driver. I told him that I thought I could handle either position so would do whatever he thought was best. Several days after that, our platoon sergeant called me over and told me that I had been appointed as his driver.

In early June we went out on a night blackout march. After sitting around the motor park all afternoon and evening until 10 P.M., we finally moved out on the march. Needham drove and I was in the assistant driver's seat. I hadn't driven enough to try the night blackout march. It was very difficult to see the very small dim red taillight on the tank in front of you, especially with swirls of dust between it and you. It was a good experience, though, and the following morning we were assigned a new objective.

After securing the objective, we went back to the motor park, where we performed first-echelon maintenance such as filling the gas tank, greasing the bogie wheels, and so forth. (Bogie wheels are made of metal and have rubber padding on the outer surface. They are the small supporting wheels that roll on the inside of the track as it is laid on the roadway. They are part of the suspension system of the tank.) We were working away when all of a sudden we heard a loud explosion. We ran over to the Company C area where we had heard it. There lay a lieutenant in front of a tank with his left arm torn off below the elbow. Also, his left side was badly injured and peppered with shrapnel. They called the medics right away, but by the time the ambulance arrived, the lieutenant was already dead. It was a horrible sight.

The lieutenant had picked up a shell out in the field which he thought was an armor-piercing shell, but it had turned out to be a high-explosive shell. Armor-piercing shells burn their way through the steel hull and then explode, whereas the high-explosive shell, even when jarred, can explode and release bits of shrapnel in all directions. The lieutenant was completely to blame, as we had been repeatedly warned not to do just what he had done. Even so, it should not have happened.

In July, we were assigned a one-day simulated battle to execute. It was my first experience at driving in a field exercise. The fact that the company commander had assigned me as a tank driver caused some concern among the men with longer experience in the company. Their thought was that by rights such positions should go to the older men who knew tanks through and through. I understood their concerns. However, I thought that those men who hadn't advanced in rank after two years of experience would not likely be chosen for those positions. I was determined to try my hardest to justify being named a driver and at the same time be considerate of their feelings. It worked.

With all of the events that were happening at this time, I wrote to my folks, "We are getting new men all of the time now. It makes us believe that we will be going over before too much longer. If we do go overseas and I get 'bopped off,' you are entitled to six months of my pay plus all that they owe me at the time, but you have to apply. Please remember this."

A little later I was assigned to a detail to build waterproof boxes in which to pack our machine guns so they could be returned to a supply depot. We were to receive new ones with new tanks overseas. The next day, we worked for hours painting the tank and getting it ready to turn in within two weeks. Something was surely going on.

The pace began to speed up. In the first week of August, we were restricted to the base, and our classes and duty hours were extended to 9 P.M. Some of the sessions were set up for us to receive new equipment. We turned in our shoes and received new boots in exchange. The boots were strange looking. In the typical boot, the leather on the outer surface is smooth and the leather on the inner surface is rough. These new army boots were the opposite of that with smooth leather on the inside surface and rough leather on the outside. There was a consolation, though. We couldn't be given a demerit, since it was impossible to shine the rough leather. As it turned out, the rough leather on the outside was a perfect sponge for water, which was not so good in snow and wet weather. We also received new tanker overalls, cloth helmets that had a strap that snapped under our chin, new fatigue suits, and new metal helmets and plastic liners.

Then we began to have classes on reading French and German maps. We were taught some spoken French and a small amount of spoken German. Pat McCue's new bride was working in the post quartermaster, and she told Pat that our orders had been received. We would soon be moving to a port of embarkation near Boston or New York City. Our new tanks had already been sent to Camp Shanks, New York, where an advance party from our division took delivery of them and arranged to have them sent to a seaport for shipment.

For some time, several of us had been hoping to get a pass to go to the Army Rest Camp on the coast of the Pacific Ocean at Santa Monica. One weekend, four of us unexpectedly received passes plus transportation in the back end of an army truck. It was not the most comfortable way to go, but it was inexpensive. We arrived in Santa Monica in the early evening, checked into the camp, and decided to go to the Hollywood Canteen to see what entertainment was going on. One of the most sought-after orchestras in 1943 was Kay Kyser's orchestra, and there they were. What a treat for us! Since none of us was 21 years old, we were only allowed to buy nonalcoholic drinks.

Following that, another celebrity, one of the singing King Sisters, entertained us. One of our group, Wayne Van Dyke, was able to arrange dates for us, so after we left the Hollywood Canteen, we picked up our dates and went to Casino Gardens, another hangout for servicemen. Some band that we had never heard of was playing when we arrived, but all of a sudden things changed. We looked up and another extremely popular orchestra, the Harry James Orchestra, was playing. Boy, could Harry James make that trumpet perform! We could hardly believe our luck that night. Four very tired but happy soldiers returned to Camp Cooke on Sunday night.

The pace toward our departure continued to quicken, and in early September we left Camp Cooke for a port of embarkation.

5

Going Abroad

By early September 1944, we had been at Camp Cooke, California, for six months. After this period of intense training, bivouacs, combat simulation, and several inspections by high-ranking generals, the 11th Armored Division was declared ready for overseas movement. Somehow we had become melded together.

The 600 men of the 41st Tank Battalion completely filled the two troop trains comprised of Pullman sleeper cars and dining cars which left Camp Cooke on September 12, 1944. Each train took a different route across the United States. The train I was on left Camp Cooke, traveled south to Los Angeles, and then took an eastward route across Arizona, New Mexico, and Texas. It left Texas at the northeast corner, went across Arkansas, and then turned south into Mississippi, completely bypassing Louisiana. We wondered if this was to miss the congestion caused by the number of army and navy installations there. In Mississippi we turned east and crossed Alabama to Atlanta, Georgia, before heading north to New Jersey. The heat of summer was still with us. Since our train car had no air-conditioning, we had to keep the windows open to get any air movement. Once again we found ourselves covered with soot from the coal-fired steam engine. Our destination was the port of embarkation at Camp Kilmer, New Jersey.

Censoring of our mail was begun when we boarded the train to prevent the leak of any information that might be helpful to the enemy. Each letter that we wrote was left unsealed and turned into the first sergeant. The company officers read every outgoing letter and blacked out any wording that might give classified or secret information. This was to continue until VE Day, May 8, 1945.

We arrived at New Brunswick, New Jersey, after a long, hot ride of five days and nights. At Camp Kilmer, we were kept occupied by lengthy marches and calisthenics routines on the golf course of nearby Rutgers University. We were each given several two- and three-day passes while waiting to board a ship.

From Camp Kilmer, it was an easy train ride to Washington, D.C., where I visited my sister. Her husband had already been sent to the Pacific. I also visited his parents in New York City. While his mother cooked delicious meals for us, his dad showed me the city and how to get around on the subway. We saw many of the sights, including the Empire State Building, where we were allowed to go out on the balcony surrounding the top floor. What a thrilling sight it was to look out over New York City! A small-town boy from Iowa could hardly imagine all of this existed.

On the afternoon of September 29th, we dressed in long johns and woolen olive-drab uniforms. Each of us packed personal items in a musette bag (a small backpack that would stay with us on the ship), put the strap over one shoulder, and marched a mile and a half in the sweltering heat from Camp Kilmer to the train station. Our duffel bags had been sent directly to the ship on army trucks and would not be available until we disembarked at our destination site.

The train took us to Jersey City, where we boarded a ferry, crossed the Hudson River, and landed at New York City's Pier 88. Awaiting us there was a British ship, the HMT *Samaria* (His Majesty's Transport *Samaria*). At the pier, we were given coffee and doughnuts by the Red Cross while an army Negro band played popular tunes. Then we boarded the ship and were directed to our quarters. The only visitor at Pier 88 that night was Postmaster General Frank C. Walker, father-in-law of Captain Robert Ameno, our company commander. Other than that, we thought we were a deep, dark secret.

Our quarters were in an old dining room in the center of the ship. We slept in hammocks hung from ceiling hooks over stationary tables. With no portholes, it was still sweltering hot. We settled ourselves (about seventy men in a 20 × 30–foot room) as comfortably as possible. We were required to wear our life jackets at all times and were not allowed to be on deck after dark. That night was no exception, so we were all asleep in our quarters below deck when, a little after midnight, the *Samaria* slipped away from the dock and sailed down past the Statue of Liberty and into the dark blue waters of the Atlantic. When we went on deck the following morning, we found that we had joined a huge convoy sometime during the night. We were surrounded by all manner of Allied ships.

We were told that our convoy was the largest ever to cross the Atlantic. Looking in any direction from our deck, I could see no end to foc'sles of ships. Destroyers and sub chasers moved in and around us all the time. In addition, aircraft carriers in our convoy provided overhead air protection. The sixth day out, we saw the submarine chasers rolling barrels of high explosives off their decks. We were told later that a submarine had been stalking us but that the depth charges had gotten it.

The *Samaria* had been one of the Cunard White Star Line's finest ships until they built the original *Queen Elizabeth* and the *Queen Mary.* You could tell it had been quite a ship in its day; it even had an elevator to ride between decks. There was no question, though, but that it had seen better days. There were large areas on the bulkheads where the paint was chipped off. The elevator was ancient even by the standards of 1944, and the air-handling system was pretty inadequate.

With 5,000 soldiers on board, the ship was very crowded. The showers used salt water, so we always felt sticky when finished. That fact discouraged many of us from taking frequent showers. Our quarters constantly smelled like a locker room in a gymnasium.

We were surprised to learn that we were to be fed only two meals a day, a pretty severe measure for growing boys. The hot food served to us was cooked in a steam cooker and was absolutely awful. I asked to go on permanent KP duty so I could eat decently, that is, the food that the crew and our officers ate. KP duty involved taking large pots of steamed food to our quarters. We served the food directly into each soldier's mess kit. We provided tubs of hot water for each soldier to wash and rinse his own mess gear. After serving our company, we were allowed to go back to the kitchen and eat our meals.

Other than an hour of calisthenics each morning, there was little in the way of army duty to keep us occupied each day, so we spent most of the time on the deck reading and visiting with fellow soldiers. One of the soldiers, the chaplain's assistant, had a banjo which he seemed to strum at every waking hour. He was from the hills of Tennessee and mostly sang mountain ballads and folk music. We gradually learned words to some of the songs and joined in the singing. An all-time favorite was "I Saw a Wreck on the Highway, But I Didn't Hear Nobody Pray."

Once we were at sea, we learned that we were to land at Cherbourg, France. Sometime en route, however, our destination was changed to Liverpool, England. The two-week voyage was mostly uneventful. When we arrived at the dock in Liverpool, there was a large crowd awaiting us. They turned out to be the families of our ship's British crew, who told us that the Germans had reported our ship sunk three days out from port. One of the families informed us that this was the fourth time that the Germans had reported the *Samaria* sunk.

The most noticeable thing about Liverpool was the damage to docks and buildings as a result of the bombing. We disembarked and were directed to a train that was sitting on the dock tracks. We were fascinated by the train car, as it had no open coaches and no center aisle. Instead, there were eight compartments to a car and each was entered directly from an outside door. In every compartment were two opposing seats, each seating five or six persons. After leaving Liverpool, our train took us through the English countryside, which was green and lush from frequent rains. The villages we passed through were neat and clean looking. Our special train took us directly to Warminster on the Salisbury Plain in southwestern England. We were met by army trucks and taken to a small camp in the village of Longbridge Deverill. The camp was right in town and was pretty spartan, much like the old Civilian Conservation Corps camps in the United States.

6

England

The day after our arrival in Longbridge Deverill was Sunday, so several of us went to the village church for the morning service. The church was a handsome stone building dating back to the thirteenth century and had been consecrated by Thomas à Becket. The pipe organ was hand pumped and nicely tuned. We enjoyed the Church of England service and noted the similarities between it and the Episcopal service.

A few days later, we were moved by trucks to nearby Tilshead, where there was a large armored center for the British army. Surrounding it were broad expanses of land suitable for field training and tank maneuvering in addition to repair and maintenance facilities for the tanks. A plus for us there was a movie theater and other recreation facilities. Shortly after moving to Tilshead, we received our new Sherman tanks, which had come to England on another ship in our convoy.

All of the tank weapons and their component parts were made of polished metal and came packed in wooden boxes. In order to keep them from rusting in the salty sea air, they had been coated with Cosmolene, a very oily wax material. The best way to remove Cosmolene was to dip the coated parts in boiling water until the material melted off. For days on end, we filled large metal drums with water, brought the water to a boil over a coal fire under the drum, and then immersed the coated parts in the boiling water. After the Cosmolene melted off, the part was dried, coated with light oil, and ready for installation in the tank. This process of getting the equipment ready for the entire tank took three weeks of tedious work. We had begun to assume that the rainy season was all the time, as we cleaned most of the Cosmolene off the weapons in the rain. Rain or shine, though, we carried out our normal activities.

During that period, we also gave each tank a name and stenciled it on both sides of the hull. Our tank was named Phikeia, meaning "chosen." Lack of space inside the tank made it necessary for us to place some of our belongings elsewhere, so our mechanics welded half-inch steel rods around the outside of the turret. This gave us a place to hang our musette bags and sleeping bags. It was a very handy arrangement.

After getting our new tanks cleaned up and ready for action, we had about six weeks of maneuvers to learn their ins and outs. We found them to our liking when compared to the old models that we had at Camp Cooke. Because they were new, they were much cleaner than anything we had previously known. The hulls of these tanks were made of two-and-one-half-inch-thick steel plates welded together. This seemed like great protection until we saw the German tanks in action several months later.

The engine of the new Sherman was made by welding two Ford V-8 engines together. It was water cooled and generated 600 horsepower. Even though there was still a manual gear shift, it was easy to drive, as the gears were very well meshed. This tank took two gallons of gas to go one mile, just like the old ones at Camp Cooke, but this one was far more powerful. In the turret, a 75mm gun was the major firepower. Not having been in combat yet, we were not aware of the serious inadequacy of this gun.

In early October, Pat McCue and I were given passes to London. We left Tilshead at noon on a Thursday, and since it was the first time we had had to make our own travel arrangements, we were a bit confused with the train system. However, we did manage to catch the correct train and arrived in Paddington Station. There, we were advised to take the tube (subway) to go to the American Red Cross at Piccadilly Circus. We were impressed with the tube, as it was so much cleaner and nicer than the New York subways. In the lower depths of the tube stations, we saw rows and rows of people sleeping and realized that they were using this as their bomb shelter.

We found the American Red Cross in Piccadilly Circus, where we were assigned to Milestone House, a hotel some distance away. The best way to Milestone House was by bus, so we went back out into Piccadilly Circus, which was now in total darkness because of air-raid blackouts. Because of this, all vehicles traveling at night were required to use tiny white lights in the front and equally small red lights in the rear. They were very hard to see at street level, so they must have been extremely hard to see from the air. We boarded a bus which let us off at Milestone House, a nice hotel run for soldiers by the American Red Cross. There we found clean sheets and pillows on the beds. How nice it was to sleep on real bedding instead of in our sleeping bag on a straw mattress at Tilshead! Air-raid precautions were strictly adhered to, but even so, we were pleased that there was no air raid while we were there.

After breakfast the following morning, we took an early tour of London in order to learn where we were and how to get around. The destruction of buildings from German bombing was incredible, and yet we found the English people cheerful and pleasant. We saw many of the sights in London, including Westminster Abbey, Number 10 Downing Street (home of Prime Minister Winston Churchill), and the Victoria and Albert Museum. Inside St. Paul's Cathedral, we were surprised to see one area roped off to keep people from getting near an unexploded bomb. We were fascinated with it all.

Later, we went to Harrod's, the famous department store, to look around for possible Christmas gifts. I purchased a beautiful Royal Doulton cake plate for my mother. It was ivory-colored bone china with floral decorations in real gold. It cost six pounds. I knew it was expensive but had no idea how expensive, as we were still learning the English currency. There were twenty pennies to a shilling and twelve shillings to a pound. One pound was worth four dollars. Even though it was wartime, the store arranged to send it to her in a specially built wooden box and have it arrive in time for Christmas. She was ecstatic over the plate, which we have to this day and use on special occasions. After two days in London, we returned to our camp very pleased with our experiences and hoping to return.

By this time, we were having regular road marches with our new tanks and steadily becoming more familiar with them and their capabilities. We were also practicing simulated cross-country attacks.

A month after our first London visit, Patrick McCue and I again received passes to London. On the train, we discussed the possibility of going to Oxford sometime. At Paddington Station, we asked a guard when the next train would be leaving for Oxford. When he said that one was leaving in half an hour, we decided to get tickets and go. Arriving in Oxford in late afternoon, we went to the Red Cross, where we were assigned rooms at the Clarendon Hotel, which was modest, nice, and clean. After supper, we wandered out into the town. All of the colleges of Oxford University were within walking distance.

The following morning we took a walking tour of the city with an excellent guide from the English-Speaking Union, who knew Oxford in great detail. There had been no war damage in Oxford. During the tour, she mentioned that because of wartime restrictions, the annual Oxford-Cambridge rugby football match had to be moved away from a population center and would be held that afternoon in the Oxford University Stadium. We knew nothing about rugby, but we went and were able to pick up the sense of the game and enjoy ourselves. We were having such a good time that we decided not to go back to London but to return directly to camp from Oxford the following day.

Several weeks after arriving in England, our platoon sergeant, in whose tank I was the driver, became nasty and made life miserable for the entire platoon. I wanted to get out of his crew, but there seemed to be no way to accomplish that. He took a particular dislike for my buddy, Patrick McCue, and me. McCue was quick with his wit and, without meaning to, would say something that upset the sergeant, who would then become livid. Between the platoon sergeant and the ever-present rain we were constantly depressed.

The situation became so bad that I decided to take a chance and tell our company commander, Captain Ameno. The sense of desperation overcame my fear that I might get into trouble for doing such a thing. One Saturday night, I went over to the officer's quarters, found Captain Ameno's room, and knocked on the door. He answered, was very pleasant, and invited me in. I told him of the problems in our platoon and asked if there were a way that some of us could be moved to another platoon. He said that he had become aware of the problem, but because of our imminent move to the Continent thought it would not be wise to make changes so close to probable combat. He said that he would take care of matters at a later time. As ill fortune would have it, Captain Ameno was killed on our first day in battle when his tank was hit by a German antitank missile. The problem with the platoon sergeant took care of itself a little later.

After being declared ready for movement to the Continent, we left Tilshead, England, on December 17th in combat-ready vehicles. The rain was coming down in heavy sheets. When the tank was moving fast, twenty-five to thirty miles an hour, the tank driver had to raise his seat and sit with his head out of the hatch for adequate vision. There was no way to avoid getting drenched. The rain never let up as we drove eighteen tanks in convoy sixty miles to Weymouth on the English Channel.

Awaiting us there were five LSTs (landing ship tanks). These ships were specifically designed to load and unload tanks and other vehicles onto and from the beach. Each side of the V-shaped prow (pointed front of the ship) was hinged at its base. An electric motor controlled the sides of the prow and swung them outward. This created an opening from which a bridge dropped down to the beach. To load the LST, each tank backed from the beach onto this bridge and into the hold. The unloading process was the reverse.

We loaded our tanks on the LSTs and, before leaving port, spent two nights in the guest quarters sleeping on real beds. Compared to army life, that time with the navy was sheer luxury. We passed the time reading books and magazines. We even saw a couple of movies while on board. The food was excellent and the navy cooks seemed to bake fresh bread constantly. It was a nice respite from the army.

Probably our greatest find in England was fish and chips. The fish was fried codfish, and the chips were what we knew at home as French fries. They were two items that were not scarce, were inexpensive, and made a wonderful meal.

We were very impressed with the English people and how they had proved their mettle through the bombings and other wartime suffering.

7

Forced March across Northern France

On the night of December 19, 1944, we sailed from England. While on board the LST, we were told that our orders were to go to L'Orient and St. Nazaire, cities on the southwest coast of France, where we were to contain or eliminate an isolated pocket of German troops. Since these cities were on the Atlantic coast, the Germans had been able to bring in necessary supplies by ship and thus hold on to their position. This mission sounded interesting and did not appear to have the same dangers that would be associated with outright combat.

We arrived in Cherbourg harbor the next day, but for reasons unknown to us, we were not allowed to disembark from the LST until the following morning. Our battalion of eighty tanks and some twenty other vehicles left the ship and moved in convoy along the highway for thirty miles to the small resort village of Barneville on the west coast of the Cotentin Peninsula, where we camped.

While doing maintenance on our tank, we discovered that one of the two radiator fans, which were enormous things for an engine that size, had broken its anchoring bolts and was loose. This required immediate attention. Our company mechanics welded new bolts onto the rear of the engine compartment, to which we fastened the frame of the fan. That created a very stable connection.

It was here that we learned that our orders had been changed and that we would not be going to the southwest of France. A German breakthrough had occurred in the Ardennes region of Belgium and Luxembourg. The 11th Armored Division was to be ready to move at a moment's notice on a forced march to the front in Belgium, where we would enter battle to stop the advance of the German troops. This change unnerved all of us, as a move to the western battlefront sounded much more ominous than did the previous orders to the southwest of France.

We were told that there was a critical shortage of transportation needed to carry supplies of all types to the battlefront. So we were asked to fill the storage compartments of the tank with ammunition for the 75mm gun and the .30-caliber machine guns before leaving Barneville. We also filled our storage cabinets with K-rations (boxes with cans of potted meat and crackers), C-rations (small cans of beans, meat, or ham and potatoes, etc.), and D-rations (dreadful-tasting chocolate bars that would melt only in high heat). The turret crew (tank commander, gunner, and loader) loaded these items while the assistant driver and I worked on securing the radiator fan. We had filled our tank with cookies and candies from our Christmas boxes as well as gum from PX rations. We also filled one duffel bag with items belonging to the entire crew and hooked it along with our musette bags and our sleeping bags on racks welded onto the outer sides of the turret. This saved space inside the tank.

It was a very short night, as we worked on the radiator fan until well after midnight before going to bed in our sleeping bags out on the cold ground. Before daybreak the next morning we were up, had breakfast, and were prepared to respond to a change in plans. Following new orders, on December 22nd, the 41st Tank Battalion began a 450-mile forced march across northern France through St. Lo, Falaise, and Paris to Soissons. The weather was freezing and those tanks were cold, cold. There was no way to keep warm in a moving Sherman tank in the winter.

Cherbourg had been our introduction to the French. They were friendly, but not overly so. Not until we moved on into inner France did we find a more open and receptive people. In addition to the destruction seen at St. Lo and Falaise, many of the villages were also leveled. Even the churches had not escaped damage. People were living in remnants of old buildings. I had thought the English had undergone so much, but then to see the massive destruction everywhere in France was unbelievable. The countryside, though, was beautiful and pastoral. The villages were quite similar in appearance to those in England.

We drove steadily all day and on the first night stopped near Falaise to refuel, provide necessary maintenance for the tanks, and try to sleep. The second night we stopped at an airfield outside of Mantes. This had been German Reichsmarschall Hermann Goering's favorite airfield in occupied France.

Early on the morning of December 24th, we stopped on the outskirts of Paris to refuel. The French people came out of their homes in large numbers, bringing with them wine, cognac, and giant pears to give us. We found the pears delicious and the cognac very warming. On the outskirts, Paris looked very much like a typical village, but it developed into a large metropolis as we moved on into the inner city. Modern apartments, people wandering about, subway entrances, and beautiful girls all met the eye. An old lady walked up to the tank in front of us and handed them a bottle of wine and a baguette of French bread. Everyone stopped to wave us through. It made us feel good that they were so happy to see us.

Their clothes looked quite worn, as might be expected, but all of the people had a bright and hopeful look. As we slowly moved on through Paris, people kept bringing bread and wine. They were so insistent, how could we possibly refuse?

Before leaving England, we had been allowed to buy extra supplies at the Post Exchange, so I had a cache of goodies. After seeing these poor French kids who would doubtless have no visit from Santa that year, I threw them all of the packs of gum and most of the candy that I had. It was wonderful to see the excitement of the children catching the candy and gum. That was reward enough.

Despite the warm greeting we received in Paris, we had to keep moving to reach our destination of Soissons before dark. As we neared Soissons, we passed two beautifully kept United States Military Cemeteries. That really gave me pause. Would we end up in one of those places?

Just then, we blew a bogie wheel. This was the expression we used when the bogie wheel's rubber padding got hot, separated from the metal rim of the wheel, and blew off. The bogie wheels rolled on the inside of the lower track. They provided the support between the tank hull and the tank tracks and were an essential part of the suspension system of the tank. (See side of Sherman tank in the illustration on page 25.) The tank track could be damaged if the rough bogie wheel rode on the track too long. The blown bogie also created a rough ride in the tank. The bogie wheels were one of the most vulnerable mechanical parts of the Sherman tank. We were not too far from our destination, so we decided to keep rolling until we got there.

It was Christmas Eve, and we had finally arrived at Soissons. We pulled into the yard of the vacant hospital where we were to spend the night. At that time, this march from Cherbourg to Soissons was reputed to be the longest forced march culminating with entry into battle in American military history.

After changing the bogie wheel and performing maintenance on the tank, we got to bed late. About thirty minutes later, a Kraut plane that we nicknamed "Bed Check Charlie" spotted our vehicles and started firing at our tanks. We woke up to the sound of Charlie's machine-gun firing followed by a small blast. Although the strafing and a single dropped bomb did no harm, this was our first combat experience, so it left us with the heebie-jeebies.

Soissons had been beautiful at one time, and despite its war damage, it looked interesting. We saw a lovely old abbey with moonlight shining through its damaged spires. It still held a certain air of enchantment. I decided that I would like to see it again after the war.

At Soissons, we learned that we had become part of the U.S. Third Army under the command of General George S. Patton. We were informed about some of the Third Army rules. One was that we were required to wear a *tie* at all times, including when in battle. Another rule was that we were to wear our helmets any time we were outside the tank. Failure to obey either of these rules would result in a court-martial for breech of discipline.

On the Sherman tank, the tracks as designed were narrow for the weight they carried. So General Patton had metal extensions made by French metal workers that added four inches to the width of the track, hopefully decreasing the tendency to bog down in mud or snow. On Christmas Day, we worked for twelve hours adding these extensions. This was interrupted only by a brief Christmas

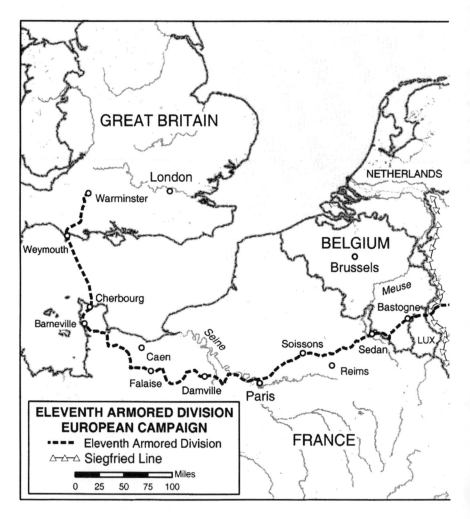

service and a delicious Christmas dinner prepared by our mess crew. They served turkey and dressing in the mess kits of a grateful company.

Around eight o'clock Christmas night, we left Soissons on a ninety-mile blackout march. I was driving and it was pitch black. I could barely see the tiny red lights on the back of the tank in front of

About two in the morning, our tank blew another bogie wheel.

pped in front of a house in the next French village to await the

overy vehicle that carried the mechanics who would change

reak, the lady of the house where we had stopped came

out and asked us to come in and have breakfast. We had been told to be wary of people in this area, as they might be German sympathizers. But our hunger got the best of us, and we accepted her offer. She prepared hot chocolate and toast for us. It was delicious. There was no problem with their loyalties. They were patriotic French and were deeply concerned that the Germans had reached a point just 100 miles east of them. She wanted us to take a bottle of champagne, but we declined. We offered her some French francs for their hospitality, but she would not accept. We did persuade her to take a pack of cigarettes, which she did, saying, "Merci." Encounters like this were teaching me that I might be missing out on some years of formal education, but I was receiving an education of a different nature that I would never forget.

The mechanics arrived, changed our bogie wheel, and we were on our way. A little before we reached our destination that morning, we passed through the bivouac site of our division medics. They were awaiting movement to the front to support us in battle. An almost uncontrollable feeling of nausea swept over me as I saw all of those ambulances with red crosses on them. I could only vaguely sense what foreboding they carried.

We reached our bivouac site at Poix Terran, about twenty miles from Sedan, France, by the middle of the morning. It was here that we learned that German intelligence had announced that the 11th Armored Division had relieved the 94th Division, which had been containing the L'Orient/St. Nazaire pocket in southwest France. *Surprise, surprise!* We were in northeastern France, 450 miles from L'Orient, ready to enter battle near Bastogne, Belgium.

8

Entry into Battle

While still in England, the 11th Armored Division was organized into three combat units, Combat Commands A, B, and R (Reserve). Each combat command was considered a complete fighting unit and contained the following organizations:

One tank battalion
One armored field artillery battalion
One armored infantry battalion
One armored engineer company

In addition, the division retained control of the following organizations to serve all three combat commands as needed:

Headquarters, 11th Armored Division
One armored medical battalion
One armored military police platoon
One armored signal company
One cavalry reconnaissance squadron mechanized
One ordnance maintenance battalion

This organizational structure provided an effective system for combat in which three separate objectives could be operational at the same time. The 41st Tank Battalion was assigned to Combat Command B. In each tank battalion there were three medium tank companies and one light tank company—Companies A, B, C, and D.

Once in the forest at Poix Terran, near Sedan, France, we assumed responsibility for guarding the Meuse River from Verdun to Givet, a distance of 160 miles. Although there was a theoretical battle line between the German and Allied troops from Alsace in the south to Holland in the north, sizable distances along this line existed in which there was no active fighting. One such area was that segment along the Meuse River to which we were assigned.

The weather was miserable and very cold, with overcast skies and intermittent snow showers. My little bottle of ink even froze. On the third day, I was walking guard when we received orders to move to a point northeast of Neufchâteau, Belgium, and prepare to enter battle. This included assignment of call names for identification on the radio. The radio name for the 41st Tank Battalion was "Poker." The battalion commander, Lieutenant Colonel Wray F. Sagaser, was an avid poker player, hence the name. The call name for B Company was "Postmaster," because our company commander, Captain Robert L. Ameno, was the son-in-law of Postmaster General Frank C. Walker. These call names were used to communicate between the tanks.

Very early on the morning of December 29th, we left the forest at Poix Terran, realizing that fighting in such cold weather would be extremely demanding. Our convoy headed north through Sedan and into Belgium.

As we entered Belgium, we found the fields covered with snow and the roads coated with ice. Vehicles with metal tracks do not maneuver well on ice, so we were sliding in all directions. Conditions became more and more unpleasant as the temperature dropped to well below freezing. After nearly eighteen hours of slow, tedious travel, we finally reached our campsite at Longlier, Belgium, long after dark. We performed first-echelon (basic) maintenance and then received orders to attack the enemy the following morning. Amid the sounds of big guns in the distance, I ate my supper of cold C-rations, rolled my sleeping bag out on the snow, and had a restless, frigid sleep for the seventh straight night.

We were up and had eaten breakfast by four o'clock in the morning of December 30th. The chaplain was scheduled to conduct brief services, but he did not arrive. We later learned that he was unable to locate us. Before daybreak, we left the bivouac area and in tank convoy, one tank following another, headed northeast through the village of Bercheux. Our column continued on the main highway to an intersection, where we turned north on the road to Morhet and moved through town to its northern edge.

At this point, we left the road and moved into the fields to begin our attack on the Germans at half past seven that morning. We entered battle without the artillery barrage that usually precedes an attack. Artillery shelling of a battlefield for a period of time before ground troops are committed was considered essential for a successful attack. Bad weather and heavy traffic congestion of military vehicles had prevented our division artillery from arriving at the battle zone in time to provide this customary support. In addition, our cavalry troops had also been delayed, so they were not able to provide information about the identity, the strength, or the precise locations of the enemy we faced.

In his book *The Bitter Woods,* John Eisenhower tells of the disagreement between the Eighth Corps commander, General Troy Middleton, and General George S. Patton about sending the 11th Armored Division into battle on December 30th. The division had been camping out for over a week in freezing weather while engaged in a lengthy road march, and the men were exhausted. General Middleton reasoned that fatigued soldiers plus the lack of artillery and cavalry support were an ominous combination. General Patton was insistent that the 11th Armored enter battle on that day, so General Middleton acquiesced to his superior officer. Our heavy losses of men and equipment those first few days of battle would tend to confirm the accuracy of Middleton's view.

As a substitute for the artillery barrage before entry into battle, we fired thirty minutes of salvos (repeated rounds of fire) from our tanks into the battlefield. This was not as effective as an artillery barrage, but it was better than nothing. We then attacked abreast with Combat Command A on the left and Combat Command B (that was us) on the right as we entered the battlefield. In a close-in fighting situation such this, the driver and assistant driver had to keep their hatch doors closed so the turret could be rotated as needed. This meant that the driver had to use his periscope to see where he was going. The periscope gave a very limited view of the field ahead, so the tank commander had to give frequent instructions to the driver and at the same time direct the firing of the turret guns.

Fighting was intense, and as I looked through the driver's periscope, it appeared to me that our company tanks were all going in different directions. We kept gaining ground though, and despite our seeming disorganization during a day we thought would never end, we did take our objective of Lavaselle. The *Stars and Stripes* newspaper reported that our ground gain of five miles that day was the largest ground gain that had occurred in the Battle of the Bulge up to that time. We had also captured over 100 Krauts. Never did I imagine that at age 19 I would be driving a tank in battle.

That first night, after we had taken our assigned objectives and then some, we prepared our defense for the night and found out who was missing. Our company commander, Captain Robert L. Ameno, and his entire tank crew were missing, among others. We later learned that all but one of the crew were killed instantly when their tank was hit by German guns. Another tank crew of five was also missing. Several of my buddies were in those tanks. In addition, there were four men in other tanks who were known killed and many men wounded that first day. B Company's entry into battle had been extremely costly.

The loss of Captain Ameno within a few hours of entry into battle was devastating. As company commander, he was the anchor for 140 men. Fortunately, Lieutenant Thomas Williamson, a graduate of Virginia Military Institute, was the officer who was second in command. He was respected and well liked. He assumed command of the company immediately, thus quickly bringing to us the sense of stability that we desperately needed.

When in combat, not only were tank crew members engaged in battle all day, but they also had to stand guard duty at night. This made us envious of the Air Corps soldiers who returned to a safe haven at the end of the day. At dusk the Germans made a counterattack, which we easily repulsed. That first night, after deciding which two-hour shift each of the five of us would take, we covered ourselves with our sleeping bags and settled into "sleeping" while sitting up in our respective seats in the tank. The man on guard was required to stand duty in the tank commander's hatch in the turret, which was kept open at all times. During the night we caught hell with Kraut artillery pummeling us but were able to hold our position.

The next day, December 31st, in fierce battle, sometimes hand-to-hand combat, our infantry, with tank support, took the village of Chenogne two times and were driven back out both times. On this, our second day in action, I saw the first dead American soldier. He was lying near our tank, frozen. How ghastly he looked. How could people kill each other in such cold blood? How could humans stand the sight? Naturally, these questions entered my mind, but in time one becomes callous to such things. Five months later, a group of us sat by a bonfire all morning with two dead Krauts lying not over twenty feet away. Funny—that is, strange—isn't it?

New Year's Eve night, 1944, we held the high ground overlooking Chenogne. Each evening our supply trucks would bring gasoline to us in five-gallon cans. Even on a day when we might have traveled only ten miles, the engine of the tank would have been running for twelve hours, so we would need to refuel. This required about forty gallons of gas. The gasoline tanks were in the rear and were accessed by standing on the rear deck over the engine. This task was the responsibility of the driver and the assistant driver. When we stood on the rear deck to pour the gas into the tank, we presented a good silhouette against a light background. Somehow, the Krauts knew when the trucks arrived and we were filling the gas tanks. They gave us a real New Year's welcome with massive artillery fireworks. Shells were exploding all around us. It was miraculous that none of us got hit. It was scary!

On New Year's Day, 1945, a well-coordinated task force of infantry and tanks supported by artillery and the Air Corps fought its way into a heavily damaged Chenogne and the woods to its north. Chenogne had lost twenty-nine of its thirty-one homes and the church during the battles. We were able to hold that village and the woods and advanced ten miles toward the objective of Mande St. Etienne. Our position New Year's night was on a ridge at the edge of a forest about three miles short of Mande.

Once again, we held our ground gains that night. The following morning, January 2nd, all was quiet and we were sort of relaxing. Forgetting previous warnings, several of us had gotten out of our tanks and were standing talking when all of a sudden, the

Krauts dropped a couple of small shells where we were gathered. This meant that they had us in their gun sights and were measuring distance with their first shells. Hearing the shrill sound of incoming shells, I took off for the driver's compartment and jumped in just in time to miss the 240mm rocket that scarred up the side of our tank.

Two of our men were killed by that rocket explosion. Through the periscope I saw the explosion catch one of the men to whom I had just been talking. With great force, it lifted him off the ground in a standing position and then laid him down on the ground on his back, lifeless. What a frightening sight. Boy, I may have hated those tanks at Camp Cooke, but I surely have given thanks many times since then for that old "metal coffin."

Later that day, an overwhelming attack on Mande St. Etienne was made with the combined might of Combat Command B. Following a tremendous artillery barrage, the attack started through a funnel-shaped opening in a dense forest. The opening was wide as we entered and narrowed as we went toward Mande. The first tank into the opening ran into swampy ground hidden by snow cover, which made tank passage impossible. Our reconnaissance troops quickly found other routes on each side, so the advance was resumed.

The Germans had placed their antitank guns in horseshoe positions around the edge of Mande facing us and had aimed them at the opening in the forest. The first several tanks out were hit and disabled. A fierce gun battle ensued for almost an hour as our tanks continued advancing. During this battle, many of the buildings in Mande were set on fire. When it became obvious to the Germans that they were vastly outnumbered in men and equipment, they retreated piecemeal out of the inferno of Mande St. Etienne. Despite the burning and collapsing buildings, a sizable number of German troops stayed to snipe and provide rearguard action. At dusk, the fires provided an eerie light by which our tanks and infantrymen moved into town and drove the remaining enemy out.

In the battle for Mande St. Etienne, Lieutenant Williamson, acting company commander, sustained a head injury when he was struck by a piece of shrapnel. He was evacuated to the battalion aid station and subsequently to England for further care. This second loss of a company commander was particularly critical, since most

Bercheux, Belgium, January 1944. Painting the olive-drab tank with whitewash to make it less visible in the snow. Photo courtesy of Cercle d'Histoire de Bastogne.

of us in the company did not consider the next-ranking officer to be sufficiently strong to provide the leadership needed in battle.

After five days of intense fighting, we were relieved by the 17th Airborne Division on January 3rd and sent back to Bercheux, Belgium, to sleep under a roof for the first time in weeks. We were divided into groups of about ten men and assigned to various houses. At the home where we stayed, five of us slept in sleeping bags on the floor in an upstairs bedroom while another five men slept in the living room. The living-room group played poker at every opportunity. Some of us were too young to know what the game of poker was, much less how to play it. As a nightly treat, the young daughter, Anna, made hot chocolate for us using fresh milk and our D-ration bars.

Our stay in Bercheux provided us with time to perform tank maintenance each day as well as to rest up. In addition, we painted our tanks with whitewash to make the olive-drab color less of a contrast in the snow and, hence, less of a target for the Krauts. The whitewash stuck firmly to the side of the tank because it froze instantly to the frigid metal surfaces. After nine days, we were very disappointed when orders came for us to leave and go back to the front.

On our first day in battle, December 30th, the division had run into units of three of Germany's finest organizations, the Führer Begleit Brigade, the Panzer Lehr Division, and the 26th Volksgrenadier Division. The Führer Begleit Brigade, often thought of as a small, intensely motivated division, was commanded by Colonel Otto Remer, a loyal SS officer and one of Hitler's favorites. This was our first known contact with the SS (Schutzstaffel). The SS was a unit the Nazis created to serve as personal bodyguards for Hitler. It was later expanded to take charge of intelligence, central security, policing action, and mass extermination of those they considered inferior or undesirable. Each SS soldier was required to have his blood type tattooed on the underside of the left upper arm twenty centimeters above the elbow. In postwar Europe, this tattoo was frequently used to identify former SS soldiers. These were vicious troops.

The 26th Volksgrenadier Division had been extremely effective in battle and was commanded by the highly regarded Colonel Heinz Kokott. The Panzer Lehr Division, which had seen devastating action in Normandy, had been rebuilt and was commanded by General Fritz Bayerlein, a very able commander with considerable battle experience. Fighting was extremely intense.

In his book *War as I Knew It,* General George S. Patton describes the entry of the 11th Armored Division into battle. He was very critical of the initial fighting ability of the division. He also expressed his dissatisfaction with the leadership of General Charles S. Kilburn, the only commanding general of the division under whom I had served. There is no question but that General Patton was a highly opinionated man who often "shot from the hip." We believed that our battle successes spoke for themselves, so did not let his comments bother us. We had tremendous respect for Patton's battlefield leadership. To this day, I feel certain that those of us in the Third Army were safer and more successful when fighting by his decisions than we would have been in one of the other U.S. Armies that was commanded by a general who had less armored savvy.

The Bulge was closed when the 11th Armored Division Cavalry troops met the soldiers from the U.S. First Army along the Ourthe River near Houffalize, Belgium. Following that, Patton relieved General Kilburn and named General Holmes E. Dager to replace him. General Patton then states in his book, "The Eleventh Armored Division later became a very fine combat division."

9

The Ambush at Noville

After rest and recuperation in Bercheux, Belgium, we were ordered back to the battlefront on January 12th, 1945. By this time, the battle line was slightly north of Bastogne, not far from where it had been when we were relieved nine days earlier. Our orders were to move north to the village of Villeroux. There had been more snow and freezing rain and the roads had become extremely icy, so our tanks were sliding in all directions. It took us fourteen hours to go eight miles.

The following day we moved through Bastogne and stopped for the night south of Foy near the IP (Initial Point, the point of entry into battle the next day). After a supper of cold C-rations and a cup of hot coffee made on the little stove in our turret, we set up the guard schedule so that each member of our crew would take a two-hour turn during the night while standing in the tank commander's hatch. Each of us "slept" while sitting in the seat we normally occupied. This was the usual sleeping arrangement when in dangerous territory.

In freezing weather, nothing can be colder than a tank with frost forming over the interior of the thick steel walls. Many of us had frostbitten feet from being out in the cold and damp for prolonged periods. During the Battle of the Bulge, this was a common problem, causing a large number of soldiers to be evacuated to hospitals in the rear for treatment. We developed our own method of managing frostbite by cutting a wool army blanket into strips three inches wide and wrapping our feet with these when we were not actively fighting. We wore the army-issue galoshes over these strips. This helped, as we could change the wrappings every few hours to keep our feet dry. Following an urgent request, my parents sent me a pair of felt boots to wear inside the army-issue galoshes. That was the best solution yet.

When battle plans were drawn for our attack on Noville, troops of the 101st Airborne Division occupied the village of Foy. However, on the night of January 13th, the 101st had been driven out by a strong German counterattack. Because of this, recapturing Foy became our first objective on January 14th.

For fighting on the 14th, Company B was detached from its usual line of command to the 41st Tank Battalion and was assigned to serve under the 21st Armored Infantry Battalion. Armored infantry were not typical foot soldiers, as they rode in lightly armored half-track trucks. They fought from the half-track, which was an open truck with wheels in front for steering while on each side of the back there was a track system instead of wheels to propel the vehicle.

The plan was for Company B to assume the point for battle the morning of January 14th with the 21st Infantry supporting. The fighting had gone well, and we had taken Foy by early afternoon. From there, we began our attack on Noville with the 21st Infantry at the point and the tanks of Company B supporting. We were in line formation, side by side, backing up the infantry and firing continuously into the Germans, who were on high ground near Noville. They were returning heavy fire from mortars as well as from tank and antitank guns.

Some of the German tanks had the extremely high-velocity 88mm guns. The guns on our Sherman tanks were the much slower 75mm guns that produced less than half the velocity of the German guns. In addition, the explosive force of our projectiles was considerably less than that from most of the German weapons. We had learned that we would almost always lose one and often two Shermans in battle with the heavier German tanks, as their high-powered guns could penetrate our tanks from any angle. Because the hulls of the German tanks were thicker on the front and sides, the only way we could disable them was by firing into the tank's rear.

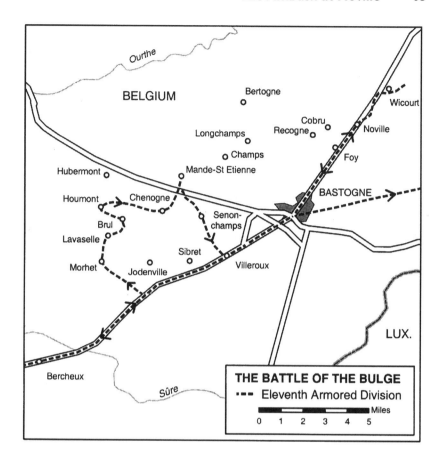

We were taking a toll on their foot soldiers by firing our .30-caliber machine guns and were slowly but steadily gaining ground. Our armored infantry then tried to make an attack in half-track vehicles but were quickly repulsed by intense fire. The German 88mm guns hit three of the vehicles instantly and set them on fire. One soldier had gotten partway out of the half-track when he was caught. He lay there burning. I almost lost faith in humanity; that was the most appalling sight I had ever seen.

Now we had to get that gun, the one that hit the half-tracks. We disabled the German tank by steadily firing our large guns, but not before it knocked out one of our tanks. The German gun had fired an armor-piercing projectile that entered the turret, killed all three men, and then exited the other side. We knew that the German 88 was extremely powerful, but this was devastating for us to see. We were later able to measure the distance from which it had been fired—1,700 yards, almost one mile!

There were dense forests facing us, good for the German defensive action but not easy for the offensive fighting that we were doing. By later afternoon, we had fought our way to the southern edge of Noville. Because winter days are short in northern Europe, dusk was upon us even at 4 P.M. We moved into a defensive position just outside of Noville and were organizing for the night when our acting company commander received an order by radio from the commander of the 41st Tank Battalion to rejoin them by proceeding through *the objective* to the high ground on the other side of town. When talking on the radio, we did not use proper names, such as Noville, but used nouns such as *the objective* that would not give away our position. To our front was the village that had been fiercely defended by the Germans all afternoon. It seemed very strange that we could now simply drive into town.

But an order was an order, so after considerable reluctance on the part of our officers to make such a move, particularly after dark, we assumed a column formation and started into Noville. We followed the acting company commander as his tank started up the narrow road. There were destroyed buildings and disabled German tanks and vehicles everywhere we looked. I was the driver of the fourth tank in the column. It was getting dark and hard to see, so I was driving with my head partway out of the hatch. There was a church on our right and a small crossroads just beyond it. As we passed the crossroads, I saw the burning phosphorus of an armor-piercing shell go over my head. Were we in enemy territory?

All of a sudden, someone on the radio said, "The tank of the third platoon leader's been hit." That tank was the seventh in our column of twelve. (The normal fighting complement of a medium tank company is seventeen, but in the preceding two weeks, we had lost five of them in intense fighting.) The tank that was hit was now burning and completely blocking the road. This meant that the six tanks in front could not retreat by that route. The five tanks following were able to back out of town.

The first six tanks moved forward on a road to the left and coiled in an apple orchard, much like the covered wagons of the old West. All of the tanks maneuvered to face outward and be in position to protect each other from the rear. By now, we had reached the high ground on the other side of the objective, but it *wasn't* the right objective. Two of our tanks were hit and disabled just as we coiled. Crew members from those tanks jumped into the turrets of the other four tanks. Two men jumped into our tank. By this time, I had closed my hatch and turned the periscope to look back toward town. I saw many German soldiers filing out of buildings. They were wearing those awful, ugly German helmets.

There was a rash of radio talk. Conversations went back and forth between our acting company commander and the battalion commander of the 21st Armored Infantry, under whose command we were fighting that day. Our acting company commander seemed to be at a loss to decide what we should do next. My platoon leader was so upset that he lay down in the snow and kicked his feet against the transmission of his tank. We later learned that the commanding officer of the 21st Infantry had planned to send some troops in to rescue us, but his communication with our company officers was so confusing that he dismissed the plan.

The assistant driver of the platoon lieutenant's tank was sent out on reconnaissance. He discovered a large number of German soldiers advancing on us with bazookas. The acting company commander decided that we would all start our engines at the same time and each tank would then take off and get back to our own lines the best way we could. We started our engines. The minute they started, the Krauts began firing. All hell broke loose, but through the grace of God, our tank wasn't hit.

I was driving. It was dark. Because the driver's view of the world is unusually restricted in the dark and when using the periscope with the hatch closed, the tank commander usually guides the driver by communicating over an intercom system. However, he failed to give any instructions to me, the driver. I could barely see. The next thing I knew, our tank had dropped into the sunken foundation of a burned-out house. It was not possible to maneuver it out.

We piled out of the tank. Once out, we hid beside a hedgerow away from the tank while we considered what to do. Our platoon sergeant was so upset that he was unable to make any decision. One of the other men and I decided that the best plan was to parallel the road on which we had come into Noville, but at a distance.

Just then, we heard footsteps. We quickly ducked. It turned out to be someone halfway running and crying, "Please don't shoot. I am an American." It was one of our men, Eugene Baudouin, who was gunner in the acting company commander's tank. His eyes had been badly burned when the turret of his tank had been hit by a bazooka, and he could not see.

We hunkered down against the hedgerow to be certain it was safe for us to start out on foot. All looked clear, so we started toward our lines. We had only gone a short distance when I looked back and saw Baudouin trailing behind. It was clear that without our help, he would not be able to keep up with us. Yet if he slowed us down too much, we could be captured by the Germans.

Actually, there was no choice. Just as we would hope to be helped if the situation were reversed, we realized we must assist him back to our lines. A couple of us dropped back to help, as he had gotten so weak that we had to half carry and half drag him. We hiked and crawled through the snow-covered fields and fences, forded a small river, and climbed a steep hill. We finally asked the others for help with Baudouin. After what seemed an eternity, we began to approach what we hoped were the American lines. We saw a farmhouse and heard voices. We immediately dropped to our knees and strained our ears. We heard the expression "okay" and hoped it was our troops talking.

Each evening at dusk, for security's sake, the password for that night was transmitted to us person to person, never by radio. Since we had left our lines before receiving the password, we were concerned that we might not be properly recognized. In the Battle of the Bulge, the Germans had dressed many of their English-speaking soldiers in American uniforms and had infiltrated the American lines to create confusion. We were concerned that we might be mistaken for those Germans.

We spent a few minutes thinking of American names such as Bing Crosby, Joe Louis, and Frank Sinatra. We also thought of words that are hard for the Germans to pronounce, such as words ending with "th." For example, when Germans speak the word "with," it sounds like "witt." When we got within hearing distance of a guard, we called out and approached very cautiously, saying everything that we could think of that was American.

When the guards saw us they called us to advance and be recognized. We went forward. The guards were men from the 101st Airborne and had been informed that we might be coming through. They had been told not to insist on the password. We were all pretty emotional at that moment of recognition. We were back among our own.

But we still had to take care of Baudouin. He had asked that I stay with him, so I promised that I would. The Krauts had mined the road, so we were not able to walk on it to reach the battalion aid station. Just at that moment, the commanding officer of the 21st Armored Infantry, Major Keatch, came by in his tank. He stopped and offered to take Baudouin and me to the battalion aid station, so we rode to the medics on the rear deck of his tank. At the aid station, Baudouin received first aid care. He was evacuated to England and then on back to the States for treatment. He completely regained his eyesight. I heard from him a time or two after the war and then lost track of him.

At the battalion aid station, I ran into our first sergeant, Lenwood Ammons, who had come there hoping to find out what had happened to all of us. He found the acting company commander and the platoon lieutenant receiving first aid. Both were evacuated to the rear echelon to receive further medical care.

I went with Sergeant Ammons to the farm near Bastogne where our maintenance crew was staying. Some of the 101st Airborne Division boys were also there. They really fed me and treated me royally that night. Our mess sergeant even gave me his PX rations (candy, toothpaste, and soap). By this time, I had no possessions except for the clothes on my back, so they provided me with everything I needed.

In Noville that night, in addition to the crews of the six tanks in front of the disabled one, there were also three members of the crew of the tank that had been hit. Two of them, Lorence and Leslie, had been injured. So the third member, Wayne Van Dyke, took the two away from the burning tank where they lay on the ground awaiting our medics. They thought the American infantry controlled the town until they saw a group of German soldiers walking toward them. They played dead while the Krauts stopped directly in front of them. They lay there, barely breathing, until they heard receding footsteps. At that point, they realized that our medics would not be rescuing them. As light from the burning tank began to die down, Van Dyke and Leslie helped the more severely injured Lorence over the church wall and into the church. Lorence felt certain that the wounds of his feet and legs would prevent him from crawling back to the American lines, but he encouraged the other two to make the try. After much soul-searching and hesitation, Van Dyke and Leslie decided to make an attempt at getting back. Leslie had major wounds, so it was with great difficulty that he and Van Dyke crawled and walked to make their way back to the American lines. At one point, Van Dyke even had to carry Leslie on his back.

The German medics dressed Lorence's wounds twice that night. They knew that they would be retreating from Noville the following morning, so they told Lorence that they would leave him to the care of his own medics. The following day, Lorence was found by American soldiers and picked up by medics.

On that fateful night, two of the men from our company, Sergeants Francis Woods and Gordon MacKinney, borrowed a jeep and went into the German-held town looking for Lorence, Leslie, and Van Dyke, but they couldn't find them. These are the unsung heroes of the war. Wayne Van Dyke was awarded a well-deserved Silver Star. Bill Zaher was the commander of the only tank trapped in Noville that was able to make it back to our lines that night. One of the tanks behind the burning one was disabled when it backed over a land mine. Of the twelve tanks that entered Noville, only five were left after that night.

Tanks that were disabled in battle were recovered by use of a T2 recovery vehicle of the 11th Armored Division's 133d Ordnance Battalion or by a Third Army Tank Recovery Battalion. They were brought to a tank recovery installation where they were examined and repaired when possible. It was the army policy not to return a reconditioned tank to its original unit because of the possible negative connotations it might have for the previous crew or unit. For that reason, we never saw Phikeia again.

My feet were really bothering me by this time, but I was keeping them dry and wrapping them with the wool blanket strips and they were improving somewhat. All of that day, January 15th, I spent just sleeping and resting. I had almost acquired "war nerves."

The next day, the first sergeant found other men from our company and brought them to the barn where we were staying. He told us that ordnance had brought up new tanks for us and that we would be sent back to the front the following day. The platoon sergeant, who was commander of the tank I had been driving, and two others from the turret crew of our tank became frightened when they heard we were to be sent back to the front. They went to the medics with "frozen feet."

Sure enough, on January 16th, three new tanks arrived to replace some of those we had lost in Noville. These had the much-improved 76mm gun that we had all wished for. And, yes, we were sent back to the battlefront. At the time, it seemed like a very heartless thing to do. I later realized that it was better for us to get back to duty than sit around with our fears.

By this time, we had lost so many men with tank commander experience that I was designated to be commander of one of the new tanks. The driver who was assigned to my tank had previously only driven one when we were learning to drive tanks back at Camp Cooke. That was a bit disconcerting. At least he had seen battle and had some experience in tank warfare. I was delighted to have Hoppie Langer assigned as gunner. He was considered to be one of the best gunners in our company. That was a big plus. We named the new tank Eloise II after the driver's girlfriend. The first Eloise had been hit and destroyed in earlier battle action.

In tank warfare, the commander must keep his hatch in the top of the turret open and serve as the eyes and ears for the entire crew of five. So, in preparation for the return to the front, I lowered my helmet as much as possible and wrapped my overcoat around my neck. You could barely see my eyeballs. We three crews with new tanks drove up to the battlefront and rejoined our company. We pulled up in line with the five tanks that remained of our original company, which by that time were a few miles north of Noville.

We had been there about five minutes when an artillery shell landed on the right front track and sprocket of the new tank. Shrapnel from the shell tore the overcoat wrapped around my neck. I even found a piece of it in my overcoat pocket! With that welcome back, I closed the turret hatch door and called the newly named company commander, Lieutenant Grayson, on the radio. I requested permission to go back down to the driver position and asked if he would send someone over to command the tank. Presently, there was a bump on the turret hatch and in jumped Lieutenant Ready as our new tank commander. Ready had been a sergeant in our company and had received a battlefield commission. We respected his battle ability.

Although the commander of the 41st Tank Battalion knew that Company B had been detached from his command the day of January 14th, that fact was obviously not registering when he gave the order for us to come through the objective to the high ground the other side of town. Since Company B was under a different command that day, it would be highly unlikely that it would have had the same objective as the remainder of the battalion.

So it was that through an error of communication, we drove straight into an ambush and were shot up by the German army. Those of us who survived are grateful that somehow we were spared, perhaps by some higher power.

That's the story of the ambush at Noville. I might add that only one of the tank crew that I was in and two of the company officers who left us after Noville returned to the company to participate in later combat. That crew member returned long after we crossed the Rhine River.

10

First and Second Drives
to the Rhine River

We were relieved from the front and sent to Champs, northwest of Bastogne, for a rest. After three days, we were ordered to the front to serve as backup to Combat Command A while they eliminated the remaining part of the Bulge. We camped a few miles to the northeast of Noville in a forest that had previously been occupied by the Germans. It was evident that they had been there for some time from the spent German rifle shells and the foxholes. The foxholes were very deep and neat and had been covered with pine boughs by the Krauts to protect themselves from the aerial explosions of our artillery shells.

While camped in that forest, we received word that elements of the 41st Cavalry probing toward Houffalize had met troops from the Second Armored Division of the U.S. First Army. This event effectively closed the Bulge and trapped a large number of German soldiers. Reconnaissance troops had gone thirty miles without making contact with the enemy. This had to mean that the Krauts had withdrawn, perhaps even as far as the Siegfried Line on the western border of Germany. The Germans called this line the Westwall.

Even in the midst of battle, there can be humor. Four of our men were relaxing while standing on the back deck of their tank when, all of a sudden, there came the wail of a "screaming meemie" (a type of

German rocket). Simultaneously, all four of them dove headfirst into the same turret hatch, a feat not possible under ordinary conditions. Even though the situation was tense, all of us watching split our sides laughing.

Once again we were sent back to Bercheux. In one of the letters written to my parents while at Bercheux, I wrote, "It is a very peaceful Sunday afternoon. Hard to realize there's a war going on nearby. This is beautiful country with rolling hills. Most of the farm homes have the barn connected at the kitchen end of the house. These farmers are all friendly.

"The peasant girl near where we stay is quite attractive and typically what I had expected, rosy cheeks, dark, naturally curly hair. She holds her thumb and index finger about an inch apart and says, 'Speak leetle English.'"

In another letter, I wrote, "You keep worrying in your letters about the cold. It isn't nice, I'll admit, but after all, there are a good many thousand more men besides me putting up with it and it isn't any worse than living outdoors in an Iowa winter."

We continued to have problems with the cold conditions and frostbite. The felt hightop boots that my parents had sent were an excellent solution for foot problems in the cold and damp weather. Trying to keep our hands warm in the cold was also a major struggle. The regular-issue gloves that the army gave us were simply inadequate for cold-weather fighting. Since the supply corps had provided us with as many woolen army blankets as we needed, I made a pattern of my hands and cut out mittens from an army blanket. The lady where we were staying sewed them on her machine in exchange for a bar of soap. Just as she had finished, in came my friend, Clate Shors, with a pair of beautiful cowhide mittens for me. They had thick wool liners inside. His mother had sent him two pairs, so he brought one pair to me. Sure enough, the very next day the army issued leather mittens and liners to tank drivers and commanders. I gave my army pair to Roy Akers, the assistant gunner and morale builder of our crew.

War is dirty, literally. While still at Bercheux, I wrote, "Today we were honored with the privilege of taking showers. A quartermaster unit of the Third Army has showers set up in tents which they brought up to us at the front. They exchanged clean underwear and socks for our dirty items. Not bad, eh? I suppose you would be appalled if you saw how long we go at times without so much as even washing our hands. It has been sixteen days since we had a shower. C'est la Guerre!"

To conserve space and weight, the government developed a letter called V-mail to be used in both directions between the United States and overseas. The V-mail letter was a single-page letter that was photocopied, sent overseas in film form, then printed in photo form and mailed to the addressee. It was a common means of letter-writing for overseas troops. My buddies and I were surprised at the high priority the army placed on bringing mail to the soldiers at the front. Our mail often came on the same truck that brought us essential gasoline each night.

To be near the front line if needed, we moved to Binsfeld, Luxembourg, in early February. The homes in this village were very much like those we had seen in Belgium. Although the local people lived in the village, the land that they farmed was at the outskirts of town and appeared to be very fertile.

We were divided into groups of six or eight soldiers, each group staying with a local family. The family we were assigned to consisted of an elderly mother and father, one unmarried daughter, and one daughter with a small son. They were very hospitable. During his waking hours, the father would chew tobacco and then spit on the slate floor. Within moments, one of the daughters would move in and wipe the spittle from the floor, an event which surprised us at first, as none of us had ever seen such patriarchal dominance.

At the crossroads in Binsfeld there was a water tank partially covered by a roof. Water ran into the tank through a stone trough. The women washed their clothes daily in the part of the tank under the roof while cattle and horses came up to drink from the tank in the area just outside the roof. Since the local women were washing our clothes in exchange for some American candy or cigarettes, I wondered how clean they were. However, the alternative was for me to wash my own clothes, so I dropped the issue.

We were in Binsfeld for almost a month while a combination of infantry, engineers, and artillery from our division cleared a way through the Siegfried Line. Conceived by the Germans as a foolproof line of defense for the western borders of their country, the

Concrete obstacles in the Siegfried Line prevent tank passage, requiring infantry and other ground troops to clear. U.S. Army, *Thunderbolts in the ETO*.

Siegfried Line ran from Alsace-Lorraine to the low countries in the north. It was made up of a combination of pylons, "dragons' teeth," bunkers, and connecting pillboxes, all constructed of reinforced concrete. By design, these barriers were placed close to each other to prevent passage of enemy vehicles and tanks. Each pillbox was so located that the fields of fire from its weapons (machine guns, mortars, and bazookas) were also covered from an adjacent pillbox. There was no area within the Siegfried Line that was not covered by weapons from at least two directions. It was a very dangerous place that could be breached only by foot soldiers after gaining control of wide, deep areas.

A classic battle plan of action usually called for an initial barrage of artillery fire prior to a ground attack. Since this was the expected plan of attack, the German defenders in the Siegfried Line bunkers anticipated such a barrage, so they were taken by complete surprise when our infantry jumped off before dawn on February 18th without an artillery bombardment. This successful attack allowed the infantry to gain control of a pathway through the Siegfried Line. The field artillery then dropped round after round of explosives on the concrete barriers to break them up. This was followed by bulldozers that came in and pushed the concrete boulders out of the way, which created a passageway for the tanks to move through and begin an attack.

Even with this good beginning, it took several weeks to clear the way for tanks to pass through so we could begin a major drive into Germany. Several villages were an integral part of the Siegfried Line, so our infantry had to take control of them also. It was the end of February before the entire division could begin to move again.

The weather was getting warmer, and melting snow left muddy roads everywhere. Those of us from tank battalions were sent out on detail to work on the roads. We were laying small logs across the roads to make them passable. It was here, while we were working on the roads, that General Patton was driven by almost daily. He was a picture, standing in front of the right seat of his jeep. His left hand held onto a special handle that had been welded onto the windshield frame, his right hand free to salute. He obviously expected us to drop our shovels and salute him, so, of course, we did.

These several weeks in Binsfeld had given us a chance to perform maintenance on our tanks, which were in the motor park in a field just outside of town. We marched there each morning, worked on our tanks, and returned to the village for lunch. Then we went back to the motor park in the afternoon and worked several more hours. There were so many things that needed ongoing attention on a tank.

At Camp Cooke, we had been taught how to care for the submachine gun and given lessons for using and firing it. In England, each member of a tank crew was given a submachine gun with the instruction that we were not to be outside our tank without carrying it. This order was reinforced when we joined Patton's Third Army at Soissons.

One afternoon just as we had completed work at the motor park, several of us began playing cowboys and Indians. We were running around the field chasing each other, when all of a sudden, one of our submachine guns fired. No one was injured, but it frightened us and sobered us very quickly. We may have had combat experiences that brought some maturity, but we were still adolescents. Most of us were only 19 or barely 20.

The submachine gun had a hammer held back by a metal arm. Pulling the trigger released the metal arm, which in turn released the hammer to strike the bullet cap. The real danger of this weapon was that even a gentle bump could release the metal arm and the weapon would fire. This was what happened in our cowboys and Indians game. The submachine gun was a poor weapon that was rarely used for combat protection.

Our cooking staff set up their kitchen and our eating area in the fellowship hall of the local Catholic church. The long evenings were made less boring by nightly movies that were shown in the same hall.

On March 1st, we left Binsfeld, crossed the Our River on a bridge that had been constructed by our engineers, and finally entered Germany. We stopped just west of Prum, where we stayed for several days while our infantry and engineers established a bridgehead. A fierce defense from German troops inflicted heavy casualties on our soldiers who were attempting to secure this foothold.

Once a bridge was built across the river, we crossed and fought into Prum, which fell to the 11th Armored Division with surprisingly little resistance. We continued the attack east to the village of Fleringer, where we stopped for the night. The following day, the weather suddenly changed to cold and snowy while we advanced to Wallersheim against light resistance. We were having a major problem; our supply trucks kept getting stuck in the muddy roads and needed our tanks to pull them out.

The next advance was to Hillesheim. The engineers were meeting heavy German resistance while attempting to construct a bridge across the Kyll River. Just as the bridge was nearing completion, we received a change in plans. We were redirected to the south and sent on a night march which ended near the town of Gerolstein, where a bridge had been captured over that same river, the Kyll. The following day we began an attack which turned into a 48-hour marathon

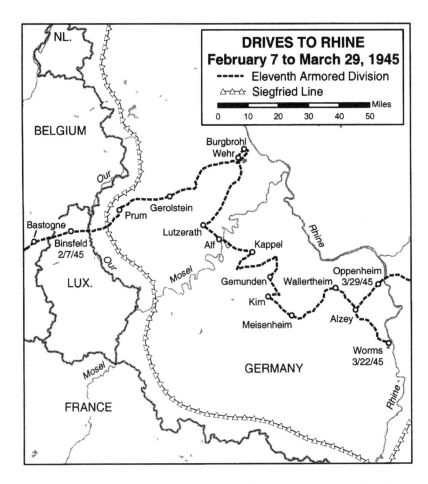

drive that brought us to Burgbrohl on the Rhine River. It had been a major communication center for the German army and was a Nazi stronghold.

"Sleep has been little and far between on this marathon drive," I wrote to my parents. "I never thought I could sleep and live for seven days without ever lying down. It still sounds incredible to me."

We moved through Burgbrohl and took over some of the nicest houses in town. Of course, the people had to move out. Ten of us were assigned to the home of the former Nazi Party leader, which was where the Nazi officials stayed when in town. It was as nice as any modern home in the States. In the wine cellar we found a case of champagne, 1929 vintage, which we were told was a banner year. Everyone except those on guard duty that night had a little party.

Our orders for the next day were to round up all the German soldiers in the area. Working with the infantry, we started out early on this mission and picked up about 100 prisoners, whom we turned over to the military police. The rattling of the tank tracks surely did jar some serious headaches that morning.

After several days in Burgbrohl, the army authorities declared this to be the south end of the First Army territory, even though we, the Third Army, had taken it. So we were ordered to leave and move thirty miles southwest to the town of Wehr, where we again worked on our tanks.

General Patton then ordered us to turn south and fight to the southeast back toward the Rhine River at Worms. On the night of March 16th, Company B left Wehr heading an attack that crossed the Moselle River and continued on a drive that smashed all organized resistance.

My crew and our tank stayed behind so that the mechanics could replace a sprocket wheel that had been damaged at the time of our reentry into battle following Noville when the artillery shell landed on our right front track. The drive shaft turns the sprocket wheels, which in turn control movement of the tracks. The mechanics completed repairs and declared the tank combat ready, so we left the rear echelon area and caught up with our company.

Just as we pulled into a defensive position for the night, our commanding officer decided that we should move on and take the next village of Kirn. By doing this, we would capture a bridge needed to cross the Nahe River. From the high ground overlooking Kirn, Platoon Sergeant Hugh Wood's tank started into town, hit a soft spot in the road and slid over the side of a steep embankment. The tank turned over several times while falling to the valley below. Sergeant Wood, one of the best-loved men in the company, was crushed to death. Pat McCue and others in the crew were injured and had to be evacuated. That was really hard, as these were my close friends. As it turned out, the bridges had been blown and we ended up fording the Nahe River near Kirn.

Our supply trucks had not reached us that night, so many of our vehicles had barely enough gasoline remaining to take them fifteen or twenty miles. The next morning we received orders to move out despite our fuel situation. Just as we left Kirn, the supply trucks arrived, bringing 300 five-gallon cans of gas. By some strange logic, we were told that we could only use it to refuel vehicles that ran out of gas. So the supply truck carrying the cans of gasoline followed the column, which had started its attack and was meeting light resistance. We began to run out of gas a little before noon, so we stopped for refueling. There we were informed that the march would continue another sixty miles until we reached Worms. We met very little opposition that day.

B Company took the lead position the next day. About fifteen minutes after we took the point, the tank of Lieutenant Grayson, our highly respected company commander, was hit by a bazooka, killing the assistant gunner and injuring Lieutenant Grayson and the gunner. We had hit a pocket of heavily organized resistance composed of a large number of German soldiers. This developed into a major skirmish that lasted several hours and ended only after they were either killed or had surrendered. We sent a large group of Krauts to the rear as prisoners of war.

After the situation was under control, we moved toward Worms. About five miles outside the city, we were stopped by our commanders and told to hold up. That would allow the backup troops from the 89th Infantry Division to catch up with us. Then together we would go through the city and clean it out. This illustrates how an armored division can get so far ahead of their backup troops that they run the risk of isolation and entrapment by the enemy, an occurrence that happened to us several times.

Together, we entered the city of Worms on March 22nd and encountered no resistance. There was massive destruction everywhere from the Air Corps bombing. We moved through the city to a suburb, where there was very little war damage, and once again lodged in fine homes.

11

Bloody Easter

We enjoyed the several days in Worms, as it was a fascinating historic old city. We were staying in beautiful homes, as nice as many in the United States, and had discovered fine wine cellars in many of them, so we were in no rush to leave. The time came, though, for us to relocate closer to the point where we were to cross the Rhine River. We moved about twenty-five miles north of Worms and camped in a field near the town of Framersheim.

Under cover of darkness, a number of Third Army units had been able to cross the river and establish a foothold on the east bank. This group included elements of an infantry division who crossed the river in assault boats and a tank company who "swam" across in amphibious tanks. Once a bridgehead was established, the engineers followed up and began placing cables across the wide, wide river as the first stage in the construction of a pontoon bridge.

Before dawn on Thursday, March 29th, we broke camp and moved to Oppenheim. I was still the driver of Lieutenant Ready's tank. As we approached the bridge across the Rhine, we found ourselves under the cover of an immense smoke screen that had been produced by the 161st Smoke Generating Company to keep our troop movements hidden from the enemy.

As we looked out across the bridge, as far as we could see there were countless pontoons lying side by side across the broad expanse

Building a pontoon bridge. Keough, *Thunderbolt Eleventh Armored Division: A Natural.*

of the Rhine. The pontoons were long airtight metal drums. Both ends of the pontoons were attached to steel cables that were strung across the river and solidly anchored on each shore. Treadways were placed on the pontoons to provide tracks for the vehicles to drive on. I was a bit nervous about driving a 33-ton vehicle on a bridge that floated on the water. As we drove onto the bridge, we were spaced by military policemen to minimize the undulations caused by the heavy tanks. I had visions of all sorts of things that could go wrong, but we made it with no problem.

Once across, we proceeded through the nearby city of Darmstadt and on to Hanau where we crossed the Main River, once again on a pontoon bridge. We headed northeast from Hanau and kept moving without any resistance from the Krauts.

We had gone about sixty-five miles that day, and our gas tanks were close to empty when we stopped for the night in a well-kept Luftwaffe (German air force) training area. For supper we had canned bacon from the 10-in-1 ration box with eggs that we had picked up in Framersheim. (Each box contained ten meals for one

Crossing the Rhine River on a pontoon bridge, March 29, 1945. U.S. Army,
Thunderbolts in the ETO.

person or one meal for ten persons.) Each tank turret contained a
single-burner gasoline camp stove, so we used that to cook our
bacon and eggs. Fresh bread with jam brought by our supply trucks
completed the menu of the most delicious meal that I could remember eating. It had been so long since we had tasted a fresh egg. We
were just beginning to realize that we should hunt for eggs each
night when we stopped.

As we were not yet confident of our safety outside the tank, we
still slept sitting in our seats in the tank. And, of course, we each had
a two-hour shift of guard duty during the night.

The next morning we started early and made fairly good
progress on our attack, even though several times we turned off on

the wrong road. Maps for the following day's battle plans were usually brought to us the evening before; however, occasionally they did not arrive. Sometimes not every road was clearly identified on the map, and often we had to follow roads that were not even shown.

Although our company was in the main body of the spearhead this day, we were not at the point. With our regular company commander, Lieutenant Grayson, in the hospital from injuries sustained in the drive to Worms, the next-ranking officer was serving as the acting company commander. It was the lieutenant who had led us into the ambush at Noville. It was obvious that the battalion leaders were concerned about his leadership, as they had not assigned B Company to take the point of the column. They constantly followed our progress by radio. Frequent communication monitored where we were and what action was occurring.

The point group of one of these columns of attacking vehicles was about three miles long. The remainder of the combat command followed the column and consisted of three more units with equipment identical to the first group. So the entire column was about twelve miles long.

Two units of field artillery leapfrogged and kept us covered on these advances. They shelled or burned any villages that resisted. The division field artillery had 105mm howitzers mounted on tracked vehicles so that they could keep up with the armored column. The heavier field-artillery pieces followed at the very end.

I was still driving on this day, March 30th, as we began our attack. We kept seeing tank tracks and fleeing enemy. About ten o'clock that morning, we passed through the village of Hartmanshain, meaning Hartman's Grove. The name sounded peaceful, but we were ever on the alert for any sort of resistance.

When we approached the next town, Hauswurz, the lead cavalry vehicle was hit by a missile from an antitank gun. That almost always signaled that the upcoming village would be fiercely defended. Sensing this, the battalion commander ordered the medium tank companies, A, B, and C, placed around the town and then called for the artillery to blast it with incendiary projectiles.

Company B moved to the north side of Hauswurz, where we pulled into formation with all tanks on line facing what appeared to be about 100 Krauts with one antitank gun and mostly handheld

GERMANY
March 29 - April 11, 1945
---- Eleventh Armored Division

weapons. They were resisting very stubbornly, but we were slowly gaining control. About fifteen minutes into the battle, I heard a loud *bang*. Our 76mm gun was really loud, so I thought it had just fired, but when I looked back, I saw the last foot of the turret crew going out of the hatch.

We had been hit again! The bang I heard was a *panzerfaust* (German bazooka) projectile that had hit the right side of our tank hull. In an instant, I opened my hatch and fairly flew out. Our 76mm gun was positioned over the assistant driver's hatch, so he could not get out that way. In a flash, he followed me out of the driver's hatch. To do this, he had to climb through a space about two feet square over a huge transmission that sat between our seats. Sitting precariously on that transmission was a set of earphones. When we later recovered the tank, we found the earphones still sitting in delicate balance on the transmission. He had not even touched them in his haste to exit. That was some feat.

As we flew out of the tank, the Germans began firing at us with machine guns. We jumped down behind the closest mound of earth, which happened to be in front of the tank. The other tanks, seeing us hit by the *panzerfaust,* backed out of firing range of the bazookas. German snipers were having a field day firing at us. Their machine-gun bullets were striking the mound to our front, showering us with dirt. I never felt more vulnerable in my entire combat experience than at that moment. Just then, one of our tanks pulled forward to get us. We quickly jumped on the rear deck and it backed away from the danger zone before the Krauts could shoot. Our tanks continued firing into the Krauts until those who were still alive surrendered. Meanwhile our artillery pounded the village with incendiary missiles, and within minutes, it was a roaring inferno.

When things calmed down, the column moved on. Our crew stayed behind to recover our tank. The bazooka projectile had cut into the track of the tank. It had then melted a hole all the way through the side of the two-and-one-half-inch-thick steel hull and cut into the water cans which were stored just inside. The cans were spewing water, so we pulled them out and threw them overboard. Then, with some apprehension, I pressed the starter button. The engine started immediately, so we moved around a furiously burning Hauswurz and rejoined our company on the far side of town.

We proceeded east twenty miles, which took us to a high point overlooking the city of Fulda. We had been warned to expect a major confrontation here, as it was one of the most rabid Nazi areas and a major communication center for the German army. As predicted, we met fanatical resistance. One of our officers was reconnoitering to determine the condition of the bridges in Fulda when a bazooka hit his tank and killed him instantly. That episode, along with the sounds of heavy guns firing in the city, contributed to the decision to bypass Fulda. Rather than fight an unnecessary battle, we went north to the town of Schlitz. A classic armored tactic bypasses any site of heavy and prolonged resistance and leaves the area to be "cleaned out" by the infantry division following. The 71st Infantry Division was immediately behind us. They moved into

Fulda and spent the next three days cleaning it out. That day we fought forty miles deeper into Germany.

Easter Sunday, April 1, 1945, dawned bright and sunny. We were detached from the 41st Tank Battalion and attached to the 21st Armored Infantry Battalion in a task force. A task force is a combination of parts of various army units representing different fighting capabilities and designed to accomplish a specific mission. The assignment here was for the infantry to be the attacking point with the other units supporting it. We were following along nicely without any apparent resistance when we came around a bend in the road and suddenly, there were masses of German soldiers, dead and dying, everywhere. The entire field appeared to be moving. It was gruesome. The infantry ahead of us had done its work very effectively.

By 1 P.M., we had conquered another forty miles of Germany. Together we killed, wounded, and captured several thousand Krauts that day. Our column had been stopped there because of the massive congestion ahead. Medic jeeps and ambulances were picking up the wounded while infantry half-tracks moved in and out to clear a path for us. While we were stopped there, a medic jeep came from the front carrying two bodies covered by khaki blankets, our own men, dead. Was this any way to celebrate a holy day? Our losses that day were small considering the amount of ground gained and the enemy resistance.

It was not our wish, but that Easter became known as "Bloody Easter" in the annals of the 11th Armored Division. We had actually outrun our maps that Easter Sunday, so we had to stop early in the afternoon.

On Monday, April 2nd, we continued our attachment to the 21st Infantry and moved forward about twenty-five miles to the Werra River. The Germans had blown the bridge at Wasungen, another indication that they would be resisting our advance. So while waiting to cross the river, several of our platoons were placed around town. Our platoon was sent high up on a strategic hill to guard the left flank. After several hours with no activity, we decided it was a good spot to set up camp for the night.

As we left Wasungen the next morning, we were reassigned to our parent, the 41st Tank Battalion, and placed in the second, that is, following, task force. We were getting deeper into Thuringia, a very mountainous and beautiful area in the east central part of Germany. And we were running into diehard Nazi opposition.

As we approached Oberhof, despite some resistance that did not stop us, we moved in and took control. That afternoon there was a limited Kraut effort to counterattack, but it had no success. We moved on through Oberhof and stopped in the woods several miles outside town while the infantry followed us into town and cleaned it out. The weather had suddenly changed. Once again, it was snowing and freezing in April. It was at Oberhof that news of President Roosevelt's death was flashed on our tank radios.

We learned that we had missed Hitler and some of his big shots by a day and a half. They had been meeting to make plans to bring Hitler's headquarters and several government ministries to Oberhof, believing that this area was sufficiently isolated to be a safe location. It was a very wealthy resort area with many large luxury hotels. There were also several German military hospitals, some of them actually located in the resort hotels.

Just five miles to our south, at Zella Mehlis, our Combat Command R troops captured the Walther Pistol Factory. This was a major catch; they found several thousand pistols and an arsenal containing many types of weapons and ammunition.

Kraut vehicles and troops continued fleeing from us, but in the process kept running into us, not knowing we had advanced so far. This clearly indicated how disrupted their communications systems had become.

At that point the 11th Armored Division was the farthest east of any Allied Army unit. We were moving so fast that we had been cut off from our supplies several times. Since we had a storage area in our tank filled with the various rations, eating was not a problem. And we had a good supply of ammunition in our storage bins. But there was no way to store gasoline. Even though we ran low on gas at times, we never ran out. Where possible, in choosing the objective for each day, we selected a town that had a landing strip. This allowed supply planes to reach us with gasoline and other essential items, usually on a daily basis.

12

Bayreuth to Grafenwohr

After four days in the woods outside Oberhof, where we worked on our tanks, we started our road marches with greater enthusiasm, as we could see the continuing collapse of the German army. We moved south thirty-three miles, a shorter gain than usual, and stopped in a roadside field for the night. After a peaceful stay, we started a drive toward Pfersdorf, meeting only light resistance.

We arrived in Pfersdorf the afternoon of April 8th, where our crew was assigned to the house of an elderly woman. Since we did not allow any German civilians to remain in the houses we occupied, she was moved to the home of a friend amid much loud complaint. Her house was so filthy that we had to clean it thoroughly before we could possibly stay there. As it turned out, we were in Pfersdorf for three days and this gave us more time for the ever-present need to perform maintenance on the tanks.

Thanks to the ingenuity of the GI, we had eaten very well for the past few days. We continued our search for fresh eggs each night where we stopped. A common sight was an American soldier carrying an empty helmet to use as a basket for eggs. We learned to ask in German, *"Haben Sie eier"* (Do you have eggs)? The substitute phrase was, *"Ich möchte eier"* (I want eggs). We usually found them in the local cold-storage locker or in a farmer's henhouse. During our searches, we also discovered that many of these farmers had their own wine collection, so the second task each night was to look for wine to have with our supper.

Our mess sergeant had been able to secure a large stock of 10-in-1 rations. These boxes contained cans of sausages, hash, baked beans, or similar items, all of which required cooking or at least heating before eating. There were five types of 10-in-1 rations. We especially liked numbers two and five, as they contained cans of delicious lean bacon. The second night in Pfersdorf, we had a banquet of fried eggs and bacon after a full day of working on our tanks.

It was here that Jules Levin received a letter from Ivan Goldstein, a member of Company B, who was in a hospital in Paris. Both Goldstein and Andy Urda had been captured on our first day in battle, had survived working as slave laborers, and were at German prisoner-of-war camp Stalag XII A when they were liberated by American troops. Up to that time, we hadn't known whether or not they were even alive. At the time of liberation, both were near death. The army flew them to specialty hospitals for badly needed medical care that was to go on many months for Goldstein and many years for Urda.

At this stage of combat, we were really moving. Each day brought us an additional thirty or more miles deeper into Germany. Our experiences had taught us that the point tank, the first in the column, had to be especially alert for fire from antitank guns or the more mobile *panzerfausts* that were hiding behind walls and hedges. When we spotted either weapon, our tactic was to speed up and shift to a higher gear, as a faster-moving target was much more difficult to hit. Speeding up in this instance meant going from twenty-five miles an hour to thirty-five miles an hour. The rest of the tanks and other vehicles did likewise.

Company A was in the lead on April 11th as we approached Coburg. We were ordered to set up camp just for the night in a field outside town to await the arrival of the 71st Infantry Division. We had not been ordered into Coburg, as tanks were not well suited for man-to-man action such as the clearing of hostile houses or buildings. Foot troops functioned much better in that role. The 71st arrived and immediately began to clean out the town. It was in Coburg that I had the first tub bath in a year. It surely did feel good.

Two days later, we started toward Kulmbach, but before we arrived, it was cleared by other troops from our division. So we stopped at Mainleus, just short of Kulmbach. We were becoming concerned that the fast-moving pace and the distances of thirty to forty-five miles each day were causing excessive wear to the tracks and bogie wheels. So during our three-day stay in Mainleus, we were able to replace some of the more heavily damaged tracks. Even though these 33-ton tanks performed well in the current fast-moving type of combat, they did require never-ending maintenance. While there, we were harassed several times by German Luftwaffe planes. They even made us run during chapel services one day.

While at Mainleus, the advance party of our division went on into Bayreuth (famous as the home of Wagnerian operas) and negotiated surrender with the *Bürgermeister* (mayor). So we made a peaceful entrance into Bayreuth and assumed the responsibility of patrolling the streets with our tanks. It was here that Lieutenant Ready, platoon leader and commander of our tank, was given a pass to Paris. Once again I became a tank commander. Paul Dunbar, the assistant driver, moved over to the driver's seat.

We left Bayreuth early on April 19th. Our platoon was at the point, and I was commanding the third tank. We passed through the infantry, who had cleared the way for about fifteen miles, and then we set out on our own.

During our fiercely fought armored battles, especially during the Battle of the Bulge, both sides lost heavily in tanks and half-tracks. Fortunately, the productivity of the automobile industry in the United States was sufficiently good to replace our tanks that were destroyed in battle. The Germans were not so fortunate; much of their production capability had been lost as a result of Allied air raids. By late April 1945, the German army was receiving very little in the way of replacements for their tank and large-weapon losses.

In many instances, the Germans were reduced to using horse-drawn vehicles, especially for artillery, including *nebelwerfers* (the rockets we called screaming meemies) and antitank guns. They still had "potato masher" grenades (so called because they resembled the kitchen potato masher), which were effective against foot soldiers. And their *panzerfaust* was an excellent weapon against our tanks. So, despite inadequate numbers of large vehicles, they still had many powerful weapons.

The guns in our tanks were capable of destroying these mobile weapons, but only if the gunner, through his gun sight, could actually see the German soldier firing the weapon. If the enemy was too close to the tank, he would not be visible through the gun sight. For this reason, we often had infantry soldiers (doughboys, or doughs) riding on the rear deck of our tanks. The doughs could react quickly to a sudden attack that the gunner could not see.

As we left Bayreuth, we had several doughboys riding on the large rear deck of each tank as protection against German soldiers firing bazookas. Before starting a fast-moving drive, we would wait for the artillery to set up their self-propelled howitzers in a position to fire their weapons and cover us in case we met enemy resistance. Once they were in place, we advanced about ten miles, coiled off the road, and waited for the artillery to come forward to our new location. After they were set up again, we moved on another ten miles. Leapfrogging had become our typical method of advance and was repeated several times a day.

Our drive went without event and the artillery had set up, so we moved out toward Creussen. The roads in many of these German towns were a maze, so the cavalry would often come forward in their fast-moving agile vehicles to lead us through town. They would then drop back into the column once we were through. In addition, we had an artillery observer, "Art," flying overhead in a Piper Cub plane, who not only identified points of possible conflict in our route but also served as forward observer for the artillery, hence his nickname. In the latter instance, Art could call the waiting artillery and direct the firing of their howitzers onto specific targets. All of this required constant radio contact.

Upon entering Creussen, the cavalry had to make a sharp right turn through an underpass and then an immediate left turn. Just as they turned right and got into the archway of the underpass, a German bazooka shell dropped short of the lead tank and exploded with a blinding flash. We stopped, backed up, and called for Art. He immediately went into action and directed the artillery to shell the village and set it on fire with incendiary projectiles. We then proceeded through the burning village with the plane guiding us. This became a common method that we adopted even if a single sniper fired at us. We had come to the conclusion that there was no reason for us to risk our lives for some diehard Nazis.

We moved to the town of Heinersreuth. Art spotted a large pillbox that we could not see, and in fact did not see, until after we had passed it. This was worrisome, but the pillbox turned out to be unmanned. Then we saw more of them, all unmanned. Why? What were we getting into?

We passed through a heavily forested area and came upon a large lake. Just then, a mile away, across the lake, out of the forest came a camouflage-painted Volkswagen loaded down with German soldiers. Our gunner, Hoppie Langer, hit it on the first shot. The Krauts scattered and ran for the lake. As we moved on, we began to see tank tracks all around us. Then we encountered "dragon's teeth" like we had seen in the Siegfried Line. None of the area was defended. What was going on?

Still more tank tracks, and then we came upon what appeared to be a German army installation. There was mass destruction of buildings and piles of debris everywhere. Next, we came upon dozens of knocked-out German tanks—more destruction by our Air Corps. Then we learned that we were at Grafenwohr, *the* armored center of the German army.

We found a cleared area where we could set up for the evening. It was several acres, flat, and had all of the appearances of a firing range. The next morning, groups of Russians began coming out of the woods after recognizing that we were American troops. Since the siege of Stalingrad three years earlier, they had been prisoners of war in a German slave-labor camp at Grafenwohr. They liberated themselves from the camp when their German guards fled. They had been frightened by the noise of our big guns the day before and gone into the woods to hide. We arranged for them to go to a displaced persons camp that we had at the end of the column.

It was here that we first saw a Russian fighter plane. It appeared to be checking on how far the American army had advanced into Germany.

In the afternoon of the second day at Grafenwohr, we started out for what was called a limited objective of ten miles. We reached that objective and were almost settled when our battalion commander decided that we would go another ten miles. By the time we got organized to move on, it had begun to rain heavily. Despite the rain, we reached Amberg, where we stopped for the night. There the infantry stood guard for us, a most unusual event. We suspected it was because we were isolated from other units and had no reconnaissance information about enemy positions to our front and sides. The infantry on guard duty is able to range widely, while the tank guard is confined to its immediate vicinity.

Our company had been in the lead position since leaving Bayreuth four days earlier and was scheduled to continue for several more days. We had the good feeling that the war was coming toward the end but were uneasy that some of us were going to be killed in one of these unnecessary skirmishes.

13

Release of
Concentration Camp Prisoners

After spending the night in Amberg, we were ready to move
out by 8 A.M., but suddenly we were told there would be a delay of
several hours. By now we were in east central Germany, where we
were meeting more resistance. Often we had such delays and rarely
knew why. We accepted the fact that it was usually for a good reason, perhaps even our own protection.

About mid-morning we finally started moving at a good pace
with very little opposition. The countryside was heavily wooded
and hilly, the type of topography where tanks can get ambushed if
they are not on the alert. As we were passing through one village,
the townspeople told us that SS soldiers were in the woods on the
other side of town. After we shot up the woods with machine guns,
we learned that the rumor was false. We had long since decided to
take no chances, so we were doubly prepared.

We assumed that many of the men from the villages that we
were entering now were serving in the German armed forces, as
the inhabitants seemed to be mostly older women. Tanks are very
noisy, and their image engenders fear. Our entry into most of the
villages was a surprise, so many of the women were crying, presumably frightened about what our tanks or we might do.

GERMANY
April 11 - April 24, 1945
---- Eleventh Armored Division
Miles
0   10   20   30   40   50

We moved on and stopped just after crossing a small river so that our artillery could leapfrog and be in a position to support us. Once they were set up, we moved out again. We did not have detailed maps of this area, and we took what looked like a satisfactory route, only to find ourselves on an unimproved road going down a steep mountain pass. It began to rain and then to pour. One part of that road proved particularly bad. It was unpaved and muddy, which caused the track treads to lose grip. Sliding downhill in a 33-ton vehicle sideways as well as forward can be pretty exciting, but we made it to the bottom without a major catastrophe. After finding an adequate road, we passed through several small mountain villages and finally reached good paved roads again.

Soon we came across an empty concentration camp, which we

learned from the radio had been occupied by Polish prisoners. From a distance, we could see the German guards fleeing. We knew that we would catch up with them eventually, as we were moving at a very fast pace. Continuing our drive, we took an excellent road and went about two miles, only to discover it was the wrong road. This was one of those days when new maps had not reached us. However, we captured several Krauts, so the gas wasn't wasted.

After getting turned around, the tank column started toward the city of Schwarzenfeld, about five miles away. As we approached, we could see that it was teeming with German soldiers. Moving into town, we found Krauts and their army vehicles, mostly trucks, everywhere. They offered no resistance but surrendered voluntarily, so we sent them to the rear as prisoners of war. Our column stopped while reconnaissance checked "the deal over the blue" (radio talk for bridge over the river). We were at the Naab River, which runs into the Regen River, which in turn flows into the Danube.

I was still the tank commander at this time. It was here in Schwarzenfeld that a Kraut truck pulled in behind our tank from a side road, thinking he was joining a column of German army vehicles. He was really shocked when he looked up and realized that he was behind an American tank. He and his comrade quickly jumped out of the truck with their hands over their heads. We searched the truck and found three pistols and other military paraphernalia.

One of our German-speaking soldiers ordered the two Krauts to go down to the bridge that lay ahead. Then we advanced toward the river and found six German soldiers in a guard house at the bridge, which, as it turned out, was wired with enough dynamite to blow us sky high. We interrogated the prisoners and learned that the mission of the truck that had pulled in behind us was to come to the bridge, pick up those men who had wired it with explosives, cross the bridge, and blow it up from the other side. However, they never got the chance. Had we not discovered the information about the bridge from the German soldiers, we could very well have been on that bridge when it blew up.

It was essential for us to be constantly on the alert for any little nuances in information. Such knowledge could easily mean the difference between life and death. This was a never-ending process at this stage of the war.

Our platoon was at the head of the column this day. We moved up the road a short distance and stopped at a point that had a commanding view of Schwarzenfeld. Two very fine highways led from the city; one was an interurban road and the other led to a nearby village. All of a sudden, our gunner, Hoppie Langer, through his gun sight saw an enemy column pulling out of a village several miles to our right. We radioed the other tanks and then shot up the whole column. It was a very odd assortment of trucks, horses, wagons, and foot soldiers. Next, we set fire to the village with incendiary shells. Then we turned our weapons to a huge house to our right front and set it on fire. Masses of Krauts fairly swarmed out of those burning places with their hands over their heads. We motioned them to the rear to be picked up as prisoners of war. The military police maintained a collecting center for prisoners of war at the very rear of our column that we called a POW cage. Those of us in the fighting column never saw it, but knew about it and of the reputation it had for effective management of prisoners of war.

We camped just outside the southeast part of Schwarzenfeld that night and kept hearing Kraut trucks pulling into our lines; they did not know that we Americans had advanced this far. The following morning our orders took us out of town to the southwest, so we didn't get to see our "handiwork" from the night before.

We continued to move through forested and mountainous terrain; our first big objective on this morning, April 23rd, was Neunberg. As we approached the town, we received word that 1,200 Hungarian soldiers who had fought with the Germans wanted to surrender to us. Just beyond town, we found them. They had only horse-drawn wagons, no motorized vehicles, and none of the better equipment that the German army apparently reserved for itself. They were a pitiful-looking group who seemed to be relieved to surrender without a battle. We sent them to the rear of our column where our military police awaited them.

From Neunberg, we headed south and were at the point of the column, progressing nicely, when a report flashed over the radio that thousands of refugees were coming our way. A little farther on, we saw a number of brown-skinned people crawling in the woods. At first we thought they were Krauts, but they did not appear to be German and were wearing odd-looking striped suits. As it turned out, they were the first of countless thousands of political prisoners we were to free that day. They had been prisoners at the Flossenburg and the Buchenwald concentration camps. We began to come upon huge numbers of them on the road. They were really holding up our progress and would not get out of the way before they had expressed their thanks in one way or another. Their joy was absolutely unbounded, and even though they were emaciated, they were cheering and waving madly.

There were 16,000 people from many nations in the group. Their teeth were black and crumbling. All of them were starving. They wore suits made of three-inch-wide horizontal stripes of white and blue. They were almost ghostlike in appearance, and they just kept coming. Some would come, kneel in front of the tank, and pray. Others would stand smartly and give a salute. Still others bent over and kissed the front of the tank. I had never seen anything even approaching this. It was clearly the most emotional scene that I had ever witnessed. By now, we surely knew the cause for which we fought.

Then we came across the marks of the barbarous SS soldiers. Lying beside the road were countless wounded and dead concentration camp prisoners. The Germans had fired at them to force them to get in our way, thus delaying our advance. I couldn't help but cry a little as I saw some of these poor refugees standing silently by the bodies of their buddies who had been wounded or killed. Next, we came upon some of these guards wearing SS uniforms and trying to hide in the village of Posing. Believe me, we gave no mercy. Hoppie Langer and I shot at masses of them. The doughboys on the rear deck of our tank were also popping the SS soldiers off with their rifles. We captured well over a thousand of these SS troopers that day and, because they were dangerous, had guards march them to the rear for imprisonment.

Still the refugees kept coming. They broke into several Nazi food trucks that we had overrun and had themselves a good time eating. They did not know their destination but just kept going. Never in my life have I felt so sorry for one group of people while gaining such disrespect for another.

Orders came to move forward to Cham, our next objective, so we proceeded. About a mile outside of town, our platoon of tanks was sent out to a road on the right flank to protect the main tank column. The remainder of the column went on to the other side of town, where they met firm resistance and became engaged in a short-lived but intense battle. Several hours later, we were called on the radio and ordered to come into Cham and set up a defensive position beside the Regen River in order to protect the rear of the battling troops ahead. We encouraged the doughs to throw thermite (incendiary) grenades into any suspicious-looking building and really clean house.

We saw movement near a culvert off to the left about a mile away, so we started peppering it with machine-gun bullets. We stopped firing for a brief period and a white flag went up. Five Krauts came out with their hands up, followed by five more. Presently, a German staff car came tearing down the road and suddenly stopped when the surrendering Krauts with their hands up came into view. We started firing on the staff car, whereupon it was quickly abandoned by five more Krauts, who joined the other prisoners.

During a lull in the battle, we began investigating the town and discovered a cold-storage warehouse full of eggs. We took seventeen crates, one for the rear deck of each tank. Each crate contained 500 eggs. Having fresh eggs once again was a real treat, but after five days of eating nothing but eggs, we became very, very tired of them.

That night our troops commandeered enough fine homes in Cham, so we had a good dinner, slept in real beds, and heard AFN (European Armed Forces Network) on a radio playing mostly tunes of the forties. In looking through the house where we were staying, I found a package of sugar and some condensed milk and remembered my mother's family recipe for patience fudge, so I made a batch. All of us enjoyed the candy even if we had no nuts to put in it.

We took an intact airfield in Cham, where a number of good planes were lashed down. Several German planes tried to land after our arrival, so we had no alternative but to shoot them down. Apparently they did not realize that the airfield was in American hands.

We had been engaged in an unusually successful campaign over the past ten days. That night in Cham, because of our recent successes, our company received congratulations from the commanding general of the XII Corps, from the commanding general of the 11th Armored Division, from the commanding officer of Combat Command B, and finally from the 41st Tank Battalion commander. It was not a common occurrence to receive such recognition.

We still had one more day at the point. What would happen next?

14

The Fierce Battle for the City of Regen

What a wonderful night we had sleeping in good beds in Cham.

Just before we pulled out that morning, our mess truck arrived and served a delicious breakfast of French toast. The mess section was composed of four men who rode in a two-and-a-half-ton GMC truck with their stoves and equipment. They were armed with only light weapons and passed dangerous spots many times to bring hot food to 140 men in Company B. They deserve great credit for their dedication and fearlessness.

About 8:30 on the morning of April 24th, we pulled out, retraced our steps to the highway, and then turned south. Our platoon was in the lead again. We reached the edge of the village of Miltach and coiled while the artillery got set up. Then we proceeded on our drive. Art was spotting for us and the artillery in the overhead Cub plane. He really did much of the work this day while telling us about entire convoys of Krauts on the roads to our sides that were trying to escape from us. He was in constant radio contact with the artillery and directed them to fire on those enemy columns. At one point, he contacted the Air Corps and asked them to send P47 fighter planes to strafe the columns. The planes arrived shortly thereafter, swooped down, and released their rockets just as they reached the

Krauts. It was an incredible sight. By destroying the enemy on both sides of our drive, the Air Corps and the artillery made it possible for us to continue our primary advance. Somehow we knew, though, that we would meet the enemy that day.

We moved onto a Reichsautobahn, Hitler's best highways, which we seldom used because they were so actively defended, and passed along the edge of the village of Viechtach. The Cub plane continued to report increasing enemy activity off to our sides. We were barely beyond the crest of a small mountain and headed down toward the city of Regen when the Cub reported that the Germans had just blown a bridge over the Regen River directly ahead of us. That meant trouble.

The Cub pilot and Murphy, the code name of Major Hoffman, executive officer of our battalion, devised an intricate plan. The infantry was to continue ahead and cross the river on the partially blown bridge while the tanks were to take an old cow trail off to the right that led to a small intact bridge over the same river. Once across, the tanks were to come back to the main highway to continue the attack. Murphy was getting anxious to keep moving, so this time he decided not to wait for the artillery to get set up. This proved to be a costly decision.

With the guidance of the Cub plane, the tanks took the cow trail, crossed the bridge, and got back to the highway. Just as we started toward town, there was a big explosion and we could see that a huge railroad bridge had been blown up ahead. Parts of the bridge were lying across the road. However, it had not been a good job, as the road was not totally blocked. Our orders were to keep moving along the highway.

Campbell, our platoon sergeant, was in the lead tank which was proceeding toward the blown bridge. Suddenly, I saw a bazooka shell hit it and explode. The tank careened crazily and ran off into the ditch. We immediately stopped and set up a line of fire on the bridges, house, and trees around us. This allowed the medics to get to the tank and evacuate the wounded men. Campbell, along with Dick, his assistant driver, and Hayes, the assistant gunner in the turret, were evacuated in an ambulance. We learned then that Hunley, the driver, and Bobela, the gunner, had been killed. They had been longtime friends.

Burns's tank, in which my friend McCue was the gunner, was designated to take over the point. Just before we started moving on, a Kraut came out of the bushes and surrendered. He had not been injured, but we were upset over the deaths of Hunley and Bobela. A couple of shots were fired at him. Then the commander in one of the tanks ordered him down to the river to wash the blood from his face. When he leaned over to wash his face, shots were heard and he toppled into the stream. I played no part in it but felt no remorse about it. For all we knew, he might have been the one who killed Hunley and Bobela.

We began moving toward Regen when a sniper hit Zaher, one of our most capable tank commanders. While we provided cover, the medics evacuated him. Then Burns in the lead tank sighted a road-block of large logs and heavy stones. McCue blew it away. Our infantry was moving simultaneously, clearing the buildings of Krauts. Every now and then, the doughs would set fire to an attic after they had cleaned it out.

This town was a tough nut to crack, as the Krauts continued to put up continued fanatical resistance. In order to have protection, the infantry could move only when the tanks advanced, as they used the tank as a shield. Casualties were mounting, and because of blown bridges over the Regen River, the medics were not able to evacuate the wounded to the aid station on the other side. Then, someone thought of using weasels, the army vehicle that could ford streams and cross rivers. It worked perfectly and allowed for evacuation of most of the wounded men.

One German officer there refused to leave his wounded buddy. We threatened him, but he wouldn't budge. When his friend died of wounds, he surrendered and was sent to the rear as a prisoner of war.

We fought on through to the outskirts of Regen. We came to an underpass from which machine-gun fire was coming. Burns was commanding the lead tank, Kathleen, and after some hesitation, decided to go through and destroy that machine-gun nest. As his tank went through the underpass, I saw sparks fly from a bazooka projectile. It landed in front of the tank, exploded, and burst Burns's right eardrum. Amid a barrage of machine-gun fire from the enemy, the men evacuated the tank and ran back to safety behind the following tanks. The Germans hit the tank again with a bazooka shell, and it went up in flames. This was the end of Kathleen, the tank, which had been knocked out three times previously. It's a wonder no one was killed or seriously injured.

One of the doughs on the rear deck of our tank asked me where my home was. I answered, "Ames, Iowa." He said, "Home of Iowa State. My home's in Iowa, too." I never did find out his name or hometown, as he jumped off the tank and went into a nearby store that had been partially destroyed. He brought out supplies of jam, sugar, butter, and wine.

Late that afternoon, a couple of the doughs threw thermite grenades and set fire to some buildings in Regen. A woman came over to one of our tanks and asked if we provided fire-fighting equipment, as her house was next door to one of the burning buildings. We took her to one of our buddies, Bill Aberer, who spoke German, and he really told her off. He took her up the street and showed her American blood and said he didn't care if her house did burn down. She certainly got no satisfaction from us.

Once we had control of the center of Regen, the artillery laid a few rounds in the outskirts, where the Krauts were still resisting. The other two platoons of Company B had quite a battle east of the Regen River on the far side of town. Buildings were burning all around us, so we kept moving until we found an open area at the edge of Regen where we could set up our defense for the night. April 24th had been a rough day, and we all felt it. We shared our rations with the doughs, as the half-tracks containing their supplies had not been able to reach us.

Company B was scheduled to give up the lead the following morning if the engineers could get a bridge constructed across the river so that the other tank companies could come across. We later discovered that there was an Officers Candidate School in Regen that trained only the most diehard Nazis. Our experiences certainly confirmed that.

15

The Intensity of the Drive Continues

Just as we were ready to leave Regen, C Company passed through us to take the lead. We were happy to see them, as this meant that we would be able to give up the point. It also meant that the engineers had finished constructing a bridge over the Regen River, so supplies and other support systems could come through. Many signs pointed to an approaching VE Day, and we were getting anxious. However, there was no way we could discontinue our offensive drives until we received the cease-fire order.

It was the morning of April 25th. Just as we started out, we passed the medics. I spotted Brig Young, a friend from University of Oregon days, and waved as we went by. As a medic, his duty was to provide first aid and to evacuate any men who had been wounded. It was always a grim reminder to see the medics, no matter how much we appreciated them.

We learned that our commanding officers were determined to rectify yesterday's situation where we were ordered into battle without artillery support. This day, we proceeded very slowly, giving ample time for the field artillery to set up between each drive. We asked them to burn most of the villages along the route, as we didn't want to suffer any needless injuries and deaths this close to the end of the war in Europe. As the day unfolded, our advance continued to go well, so it appeared that the backbone of resistance had been broken by our successful campaign on the previous days.

B Company was in the main body of the column, but not at the point, so we were less vulnerable compared with the previous week of arduous battles. In one town that we did not burn before entering, a nice house sat just ahead where the road curved to the left. Patrick Needham was driving, and as we came to that house, somehow the left steering lever wouldn't grip. Our tank rolled through the living-room wall before we could stop. I checked our crew members and found no one injured, so we moved on ahead and joined our company. I do not recall any previous time when a steering lever failed to grip. No one in the crew seemed to feel a concern for the people whose home we had damaged. It wasn't our idea to be there in the first place. We couldn't help but feel that way. We were all exhausted from such a continuous, intense drive without rest.

We had gone only twenty miles that day before being stopped because Company C had met stiff resistance from some SS troops. So our column made a bypass maneuver and left the SS to be cleaned out by the infantry. We moved on and found a clearing where we camped for the night.

An unusual event took place this day to the tank commanders and drivers. Early in the afternoon, those of us who had had our hatches open and heads out began to have severe burning in the eyes. We had noticed that the roads appeared to have a white coating on them and suspected that a caustic agent had been spread to create eye problems and slow us down. Our speed was reduced a bit, but the burning eyes did not stop us. When we ceased our drive for the day, the medics washed our eyes with a saline solution which seemed to take care of the problem.

The next day, April 26th, was equally uneventful, except when our antiaircraft guns shot down two German Messerschmidt 109 planes. We quit our drive for the night at Waldkirchen. To our surprise, we were told that we were to remain there a few days while cavalry reconnaissance went to look for the Russians. I was outside the tank preparing scrambled eggs from the case of eggs that we had picked up in Cham when a Kraut plane strafed us and then dropped a big bomb in our midst. I really dove under the rear of that tank.

The bomb did no damage, but it proved that we still knew how to take cover fast.

While we were at Waldkirchen, we were able to perform major maintenance on a number of our tanks. It was there that four of the new Pershing tanks were brought to our battalion, so each company received one. Since we had no experience or familiarity with the Pershings, we relegated them to the rear of our column. It was too bad that we did not have them when we were in tank-to-tank fighting during the Battle of the Bulge. The better-designed German tanks with their more advanced weapons had definitely been superior in that setting. Despite the poor firing power and inadequate armor of the Sherman tank, we found them mechanically far superior to any tank that the Germans had. The Kraut tanks lumbered along at a snail's pace compared to ours. Besides, we knew how to use our Shermans to the best advantage in the current fast-moving type of combat.

Company C started an attack and advanced eight miles while we stayed behind in Waldkirchen. We broke camp the next morning, April 30th, and moved to join the rear of the column behind C Company. Our company supply officer had obtained a loudspeaker and had it installed on one of our tanks at the last overnight stop. We began a trial of broadcasting messages in German to soldiers and civilians as we went through several towns.

The message, spoken in German, was, "Don't fight. Stay calm and peaceful and you will not be harmed." It may not have been translated into perfect German, but they knew what it meant and obeyed instructions.

This was definitely helping us to keep things from exploding, so we decided to use it steadily. Kratz, a friend from University of Oregon days, started addressing the people in German over the speaker. Outside the next village, we noticed that the people were scampering around frantically as we approached. It put us on the alert for possible enemy resistance, but we kept moving and passed through without event. At one town we passed through, a Kraut had just finished camouflaging his truck with paint when he turned to walk away and saw us. What a shocked expression he had on his face. He immediately put his hands over his head and surrendered.

We had followed the column for about twenty miles when, looking at the map, we realized that we were nearing Austria. We were on the highway to Linz, one of Austria's major cities. Air re-connaissance had informed us that a large number of 88mm guns had been set up around the periphery of Linz to defend it.

We were advancing nicely when, all of a sudden, a few rounds of artillery shells landed around us. It turned out to be another Hungarian unit that had been involuntarily drafted into the German army. They seemed to feel the compulsion to fire a couple of rounds from their howitzers before surrendering. The entire group was sent to the rear to be interrogated by the military police.

Lieutenant Ready was back from pass and assumed command, so I returned to the driver's position. He asked me at that time to take command of a tank in his platoon, and my preference was to serve in his platoon. However, I wasn't anxious to command, since the turret where the commander stands is the first part of a tank to be seen as it comes over a hill. I liked driving, and the driver's position was somewhat safer. Lieutenant Ready and I worked well together, so he agreed to have me stay in his tank.

On May 1st, Company A took the point, and we followed. The 41st Tank Battalion advanced across the Austrian border; we were told that we were the first U.S. troops to enter Austria. By early afternoon we moved into Lembach. Abruptly, Company A hit a heavily defended roadblock and was caught up in a battle against strongly resisting Krauts. Tragically, the company's highly respected company commander, Captain Scott, was killed there, just one week before VE Day. With his death, it appeared that B Company would be taking the lead the following day, as we were next in turn to take the point.

That night I overheard the "Doctor" (radio call name for the commander of Combat Command B, Colonel Wesley W. Yale) say, "These six check points [villages] ahead will be burned to the ground by nightfall. Those people have got to learn that resisting is useless." He evidently was bitter over Captain Scott's death in Lembach.

As expected, B Company took the lead, and we began our drive. Sergeant Bickert, with our third platoon leading, took the point. I was in the second section of the column. We moved out early and went to the IP. There was snow on the ground, so while we waited to start the attack, we built a bonfire. About fifteen feet from the fire lay two dead Krauts. Six months before, we would have shuddered at that, but this day we actually joked about them being so close.

A little later, we started the attack. We advanced through town after town and ran into a blinding snowstorm. We kept moving and reached Zwettl, Austria, where several thousand Krauts voluntarily surrendered to us. There I became a tank commander once again when one of the other commanders had an accident that required his evacuation. Although I had not planned to take such a position on a permanent basis, when I was asked this time, I decided that I should do it.

As we continued through the next village, Kraut soldiers surrendered in large numbers. We signaled for them to drop their weapons, put their hands up, and start marching toward the rear of the column. The doughs retrieved the dropped weapons. We took about 5,000 prisoners there. It was obvious that they did not want to fight and were ready to call it quits. We did not fire a single shot.

As the battalion neared the Danube River, B Company was ordered to turn on a major highway that led to the northeast while the remainder of the battalion continued south across the river. This maneuver cut off all roads from the north into the major city of Linz, Austria.

With such a quick advance, we took by surprise many German trucks of every description that were trying to escape being captured. A group of SS soldiers pulled out of town right in front of us, but we had orders not to fire a shot. It was tempting, but we obeyed orders. Later, these same soldiers came back to surrender to us.

16

Mauthausen, Gusen I, and Gusen II

After camping northeast of Zwettl the night of May 3rd, we met no resistance as we advanced into Gallneukirchen the next day, where we joined the other companies of our battalion. We were assigned houses to stay in, which meant the inhabitants had to move out. Our chaplain arrived, so we had church services in the local Protestant church. In contrast to the low attendance at Camp Cooke and in England, a surprisingly large group was there. As we were coming back from services, guns started going off. We were fearful that some sort of counterattack was starting.

Then battalion headquarters announced that all of the German troops in Austria had surrendered. This information was misinterpreted by some of the staff as total German surrender and that the war was over. Even though this was not true, it wasn't surprising that such a rumor could set off some celebration. The past two weeks had been filled with immense tension for us, as there were so many signs pointing to the end of the European war. We relaxed somewhat that night and then had very good church services on Sunday, May 6th.

By this time, all 4,000 men of Combat Command B were in Gallneukirchen. Our cavalry reconnaissance troops had been searching the area to be certain that there were no Krauts still hiding. In the process they came upon Mauthausen Concentration Camp and two of its nearby satellite concentration camps, Gusen I

Tank crew of Eloise II in Austria, May 1945. *Top:* Driver Paul Dunbar. *Center:* left, Assistant Gunner Alvin Berns; right, Gunner Hoppie Langer. *Bottom:* left, Tank Commander Ted Hartman; right, Assistant Driver Tony DeLeese.

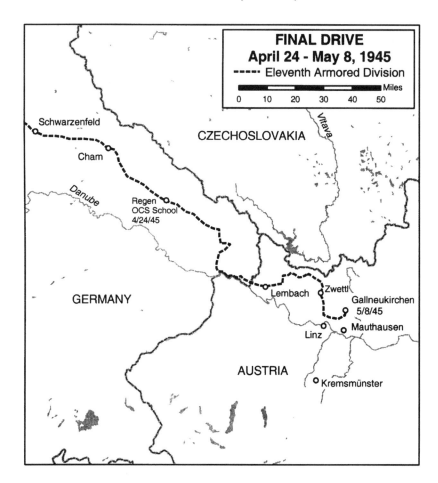

and Gusen II. The largest one, Mauthausen, was an absolutely unbelievable place where thousands of Jews and other political prisoners had been tortured and killed. It was shocking that the camps
were still in operation when our troops arrived. The crematorium
was still smoking, and there were bodies in the gas chamber.

General Dager, commanding general of the 11th Armored Division, issued an order that each unit would arrange for all of its
men to be taken to see Mauthausen Concentration Camp, so our
company commander scheduled trucks to take us there. As we entered, our truck was motioned through the gate to a parking place
near some old buildings that appeared to be barns.

Once out of the truck, we noticed a haze in the air and an awful
stench. We were first taken to one of the nearby buildings, which

Mauthausen Concentration Camp, Austria, May 1945. Human bodies stacked in front of the crematorium. Knight, *Battalion War History, Forty-first Tank Battalion.*

turned out to be the crematorium. There was a huge oven with remains still in it. What a dreadful sight. Then, just outside of the crematorium, we saw stacks that looked like cordwood. Looking closer, we realized that they were stacks of bodies to be cremated. It even looked as though there was occasional movement in the stacks. Could some of them still be alive? It was awful.

The next building we went into contained the gas chamber, which had the appearance of a large shower room. Remains of bodies were still lying in the chamber. This entire scene was unbelievable. In another building we found people who were too ill to care for themselves or had some major medical problem. Many simply lay there, too weak to move. Everywhere, we heard labored breathing. It was so sad. All of them were emaciated and wasted away. There were many survivors from other barracks who were wandering around the grounds. They looked like walking skeletons.

The townspeople of the village of Mauthausen insisted that they had not known what was going on in this concentration camp at the edge of town. But the constant stench of burning flesh had to tell them something was amiss. Our commanding general ordered the local citizens to dig a number of excavations at the camp which would serve as mass graves. Then he ordered people from the village to carry each individual body to the gravesite and place it in the mass grave. When each grave was full, they were to cover it with soil.

We later learned that Mauthausen had been established on August 8, 1938, when the chief of the SS, Heinrich Himmler, ordered 200 prisoners from the Dachau Concentration Camp to be transported to the little town of Mauthausen just outside of Linz, Austria. They were to build a new concentration camp to supply slave labor for the Wiener Graben granite quarry at Mauthausen. For two years, the prisoners worked to build the camp and the living quarters for the SS troops who would be in charge. They also built thirty-two barracks to house prisoners, but this number was totally inadequate. Once the camp was established, political prisoners were moved to Mauthausen to perform slave labor. The area surrounding the camp was ringed with electrified barbed wire, stone walls, and watchtowers. Large numbers of the prisoners were forced to stay outdoors the year round, so many froze to death.

Mauthausen was classified as a Category III concentration camp, which meant that many of the inmates were to be exterminated by being worked to death. The slave laborers were divided into two groups. One cut the huge granite blocks in the quarry and the second was forced to carry the heavy blocks up 186 steps to be transported away for construction projects.

The inmates at Mauthausen were forced to perform long hours of manual labor in the rock quarry each day, beginning at 4:45 A.M. and ending at 7 P.M. The diet given them was totally inadequate. Much of it was a gruel made from potato skins. The bread consisted of some locally grown grain mixed with wood flour (sawdust). Gusen I and Gusen II were similar in activity but were somewhat smaller. We had been hearing stories about such places and we had seen the former inmates near Neunberg, but we had not seen anything to compare with this. This enemy of ours was supposed to be human, but how could they possibly treat other humans this way?

When our cavalry first found the camp, there were 20,000 slave-labor inmates from sixteen nations. An equal number of inmates were in the Gusen concentration camps. Many of the Gusen prisoners had broken out by the time the cavalry arrived. Several of them captured one of the SS guards and killed him. Gusen inmates continued to die at the rate of 100 a day even after their liberation. In addition to working the prisoners to death, many were forced into gas chambers or lured into frigid showers to kill them. It is estimated that 195,000 prisoners had passed through the Mauthausen/Gusen camps from 1938 to 1945. No prisoner was known to have left the camp alive. One thousand SS German prison guards from the Mauthausen and Gusen camps were captured and taken to Gallneukirchen as prisoners.

Combat Command B worked to transform Mauthausen into a displaced persons camp. The first stage of the plan was to stabilize the health of the inmates insofar as possible. This included getting assignments of food from higher headquarters in addition to food obtained from local sources. Even so, the inmates continued to die at a high rate.

Lieutenant Grayson, our company commander, who had been injured on the drive to Worms, arrived back from the hospital on Sunday, May 6th. We were overjoyed, as he was an excellent company commander. By now we were suspecting that the war really was finished. He called us together the following morning and told us that negotiations had been completed and that May 8, 1945, was to be VE Day (Victory in Europe Day).

In a letter to my parents dated May 8, 1945, I wrote, "You'll never know the relief all of us feel from the wonderful news that the war is over in Europe. Yes, I know it's a relief for those at home too, but they'll never be able to feel it as we do. Officially, midnight tonight is the ending of hostilities, and I'm sure the celebrations in Times Square and elsewhere will far exceed that of New Years. Our celebration here is to be just good sleeping, and for myself, a real prayer of thanks. We are sobered by the worthy suggestion of our company commander that we think of our buddies who are no longer with us and then celebrate accordingly. At any rate, it's wonderful!"

At the conclusion of hostilities, the 11th Armored Division was the farthest east of any Allied organization and was the first unit to meet the Russians in Austria. The odometer on a Company B half-track showed that we had logged *1,000 combat miles* from the time we entered battle in Belgium until VE Day at Gallneukirchen.

The 11th Armored Division entered battle on December 30, 1944, near Bastogne, Belgium, with the normal armored division complement of 12,000 men. On VE Day, May 8, 1945, casualties in the 11th numbered 5,137; this represented 48.1 percent of the men in the division. Of the casualties, 614 men were killed in action, 40 were missing in action, and 2,562 were injured in action. Nonbattle casualties constituted the remainder of the casualties. Sixty-eight men of the 41st Tank Battalion's complement of 600 were killed in action during this time. Company B began battle with 140 men; 23 were killed in action between December 30, 1944, and May 8, 1945.

At war's end, the division had captured 76,229 prisoners in addition to the 34,125 German troops who violated surrender terms by fleeing from the Red Army and coming to us. This latter group was rounded up and turned over to the Soviet forces. The division liberated 5,012 Allied prisoners of war and 52,500 slave laborers in Nazi concentration camps—a total of 57,512—during these drives through Germany.

While we were still in Gallneukirchen, large numbers of Krauts began coming to us to surrender. They were headed for Linz. They came in a strange assortment of trucks, cars, motorcycles, and other military vehicles, as well as horse-drawn wagons. We told them to stop in a field just outside Gallneukirchen and to go on the following day. When we inspected them, we discovered that many were still armed. We rushed around collecting all types of weapons. We could have had trouble had they been so inclined.

We built huge bonfires in strategic spots to keep them in their places and so we could see them. We had to stand guard over them that night, even though they outnumbered us twenty-five to one. They were trying to reach Linz and escape the Russians. The Russians were well known for their inhumane treatment of any German soldier, but they were especially vicious to the German SS troops, who themselves had been extremely brutal in their treatment of Russian prisoners.

As soon as those Krauts pulled out the following morning, our battalion left Gallneukirchen and moved down to very nice quarters in German barracks across the Danube River from the city of Linz.

Each soldier in the Third U.S. Army received a copy of the following memo from General Patton:

VE Day

Headquarters
THIRD UNITED STATES ARMY
Office of the Commanding General
APO 403

Regensburg, Germany
15 May 1945

With the termination of hostilities, the Third Army and its inseparable comrade-in-arms, the XIX Tactical Air Command, completed 281 days of constant battle during which we have engaged in every type of combat except defensive. In each type of fighting successful solutions have been evolved.

This report describes in considerable detail the various situations which developed and the tactical combinations utilized for their successful solution.

It is noteworthy that while our operations in pursuit or exploitation have at times developed phenomenal speed, they have always been preceded by bitter and sometimes prolonged assaults. This is particularly true in the initial breakthrough at St. Lo in July, in Lorraine from November 8 to December 19 and in Luxembourg and Germany from December 22 to March 5.

The success of all our operations has been due to teamwork and mutual cooperation, to the untiring efforts of a devoted and experienced staff, to the ability of commanders from Corps and Tactical Air Commands to platoons and individual pilots. But above all, to the fighting heart of the American soldier.

G. S. Patton, Jr.
General

17

Mass Surrender and Death March

The third day after we arrived in Linz, our company was ordered back to Gallneukirchen. We were to accept the surrender of an entire German army corps coming from the East that had refused to obey orders from our command headquarters to surrender to the Russians. They were determined to be taken prisoner by the American army. When we reached Gallneukirchen, we made a huge circle in the same field on the outskirts of town that we had used previously. We placed our tanks around the periphery and put the Germans in the center of this circle. This arrangement allowed us to guard them more effectively.

Then they began to come, all 18,000 of them, including some women and children. It was an orderly group. They marched in and set up camp in a very organized fashion. We had been concerned about what they would eat, as we had no food available for them. However, they brought their own supplies and seemed to have enough for everyone. Our other concern was how to provide enough water for this many people, as our water supply was very limited. In addition, May was the hottest season of the year in this area. To solve this, the Quartermaster Corps found some army tank trailers and brought them in filled with water.

The group camped patiently for two days while we awaited instructions. On the second night, we received orders that the next day

Marching German prisoners to the Russians in Austria, May 1945. Note tank guns facing toward the German prisoners. U.S. Army, *Thunderbolts in the ETO*.

we were to march them to a Russian encampment twenty miles northeast of Gallneukirchen. That evening we informed the prisoners that they would be taken on a 20-mile march the following morning. They were told to fill their canteens with enough water to last a little more than three hours. With that information, the prisoners seemed to sense their fate. We were very concerned that we might have trouble that night, as we were vastly outnumbered. But, thank goodness, no problem materialized.

At dawn the next day, we moved onto the highway and put one tank at the head of the column with its gun and turret facing to the rear. Behind this tank we placed a group of about 1,000 marching Krauts followed by a tank with its gun and turret facing toward the prisoners. Next came another tank with its gun facing to the rear followed by prisoners. This pattern was repeated until all of the prisoners were in the marching column. There were thirty-six tanks guarding 18,000 prisoners, making the entire column over six miles long.

The women and children in the group were given a choice of going or of staying behind. Most started out with the others. We moved out through Gallneukirchen. It was already very hot at 8 A.M. We had orders to shoot if mass fallouts occurred. One thousand Krauts between each two tanks were too many to observe around curves in the road, so we hoped for the best. Just at the east edge of town, we passed a field full of German weapons and military items. This was obviously where these prisoners had discarded their equipment and voluntarily disarmed themselves before surrendering to us two days previously. We had to watch carefully to see that none of them left the column and picked up some of their weapons. They could really have given us a hard time.

They began to get hot and tired, but we kept prodding them on. After five miles, first one and then another prisoner threw away part of his pack to lighten the load. Then some of the Krauts began dropping out with heat stroke. More and more of them were falling along the side of the road. At one point, one of our least-respected officers was lashing some of the prisoners with a whip. After marching about three hours, we saw that we were approaching the Russian camp. Not only did we see the Russians about a quarter of a mile away, but the prisoners of war spied them also. There were some SS troopers among the prisoners, and they began tearing off all insignia identifying their branch of service. By the time we met the first Russian, no German soldier's uniform could be distinguished as to rank or type of service.

A Russian colonel marched the Germans into a large field that was surrounded with Soviet military equipment. The Russians took immediate control. They were friendly to us Americans, and we shook hands and then saluted right and left. The saluting seemed unending, which we assumed was the Russian style. We saw one of them using a bullwhip on a prisoner. Machine guns went off at least five times during the thirty minutes we were there. We had a good idea that they weren't firing aimlessly just to frighten the Krauts. After this short meeting, we started back. On our return, I saw at least ten dead Germans lying beside the road.

This, in brief, tells the story of the death march that we American soldiers were ordered to impose upon the German prisoners. We were too fresh from concentration camp scenes to think much about it at the time.

18

Adjusting to Peacetime

As World War II came to an end, the army had to make plans for sending the American soldiers back to the United States. Because of the large number to be returned, both from Europe and the Far East, there was a relative shortage of ships to transport the troops. The army developed a point system that would determine when an individual soldier would be eligible to be sent home for discharge. Points were granted for the number of months in the army, months in combat, months as a prisoner of war, months in the Army of Occupation, and certain other things. When points were initially counted, many longtime soldiers had more than eighty points, so they were among the first groups to return. As more soldiers were shipped home, the number of points required began to drop. When points were first counted, I had forty-one. When I received my orders to go home, they had increased to fifty-two. Until we had enough points, most of us were to be a part of the Army of Occupation.

Our first peacetime duty had been to march the German prisoners to the Russians. After leaving them with the Russians, we returned by tank column to Linz, where we settled into barracks formerly occupied by German soldiers. The barracks had been cleaned by German prisoners of war and were better than any accommodations we ever had in an army camp in the United States.

Combat Soldier Ted Hartman, 19 years old, Austria, May 1945.

We were comfortably situated with three of us to a room. We had a good little radio that picked up programs on the Armed Forces Network. The station mostly played music of the forties with an occasional newscast. In the early days, the electricity was frequently on and off, but we managed to listen to most of the programs that we wanted to hear.

German civilians were required to register a number of items in their possession with the United States Military Government, including all radios. Some families refused, so the army confiscated them. Those radios were later distributed to American soldiers. Many of them had been stolen by the Germans during the occupation of France. Even so, the German civilians complained about "their" missing radios.

Each morning we had close-order drill followed by tank maintenance. We had an occasional class on current events, including the war in the Pacific and information about the Chinese communists, who they were, and how they were different from Russian communists. The afternoons were free, so we occupied ourselves with hunting, fishing, swimming, playing ball, and photography. It was a nice schedule that was designed to keep us busy.

We had captured some Austrian equestrian drill teams when we took Linz, so we were allowed to ride some of their horses not deemed worthy of show. We rode on trails in a park along the Danube River. Most of us had very little horseback-riding experience, and those well-trained horses knew it. They loved to go under low-hanging tree branches and try to knock us off, for which they received a good swat from our quirts.

It had been two weeks since VE Day. We were settled into our peacetime routine and loving it. Each morning for over a week we were detailed to clean our tanks but did not know why. Then it was announced that a Russian general was coming to inspect us. He was the general who was in command when we returned the German prisoners to them. At the ceremony, he and his staff sat at the center of a long raised platform while our commanding general sat with his staff at the far end. To entertain them, we performed close-order drill and demonstrated some tank maneuvers. General Patton declined to attend that ceremony. Later, he attended one given for another Russian general. At this one, General Patton had the platform seating arranged so that the Russians sat at one end while he and his staff sat at the other end. There appeared to be no communication between the two generals. The Russians were clearly not General Patton's favorite people.

One night, several of us were assigned as guards to an outpost on a highway east of Linz, where we were to prevent all persons, Austrians or otherwise, from passing through the blockade into the city. Many of those trying to come through claimed that they lived in Linz and were going home. Our orders, however, came from the Allied High Command and were very strict—no one would be allowed to pass our blockade.

In reality, these people were fleeing from the Russians, and we were not to permit that. Allowing them into the American zone increased the number of displaced persons for whom our army would have to provide housing, food, and jobs. We had more than enough obligations without adding to them. One woman with two children and a buggy became particularly indignant when we wouldn't let her through, so she tried to sneak past us. We caught her, though, stopped the next U.S Army truck headed east, and put them on it. We told her we were sending them to the Russians. In reality, we sent her and her children to a camp that had been organized for displaced persons. This was one of many experiences that confirmed the need for us to be very firm with the Austrians and Germans. Some of them still believed that they could do exactly as they wished, regardless of the fact that the Americans and other Allied Forces were in control.

Barely four weeks after we moved into the barracks near Linz, the army decided that the troops serving in the Army of Occupation for that part of Austria would live in the barracks where we were staying. My company of 160 men was ordered to move to a dormitory at a monastery in Kremsmunster, Austria, forty miles south of Linz. The move would take place as soon as the monastery had been deloused. German troops had been staying there.

It was one month since VE Day, and we had already been moved twice. This time it was to a beautiful, picturesque cathedral and monastery situated in hills around the village of Kremsmunster. Krems is the name of the river that flows through the area and "*munster*" is the German word for cathedral, hence Kremsmunster. It definitely had an educational thrust, as there was a seminary for priests as well as a high school–level boarding school. The school buildings and the dormitory had been taken over by the Nazis, so the seminary students had been confined to the cathedral.

The cathedral was breathtaking in its beauty. Murals lined the walls. There were many richly decorated tapestries. A skeleton covered by a jeweled robe on display in a glass case in the sanctuary was said to be the remains of Saint Benedict. We held Protestant church services in the ballroom of the monastery. It was a magnificent room. Portraits of past kings hung on the walls, and the ceiling was covered with a brilliant mural depicting historical events. All of this was supported by sculptured columns and detailed plaster work. It must have taken centuries to construct this place without modern machinery.

A group of high-ranking Czechoslovakian quisling government officials, thinking that this would be a remote hideout where they would never be found, had come to the monastery to stay. Quisling, the prime minister of Norway, was a traitor who collaborated with the Nazi invaders and allowed them to take control of his country in the early 1940s, so the name of quisling has been applied to a traitorous leader of any country since that time. When we arrived at the monastery, the Czechoslovakian officials were having a meeting to decide where they should move from Kremsmunster. Our military government decided that issue by taking all of them into custody. A number of their names were familiar from news broadcasts during the occupation of Czechoslovakia.

The Nazis thought so highly of them that they had made available an entire freight train to bring all of their possessions when they fled Czechoslovakia. They even brought their automobiles in addition to the immense collections of loot that we found in the hallways of the dormitory. The cars were parked in an enclosure at the monastery. A number of us commandeered them and drove all over for the next two days and nights. The car I chose was a nice comfortable Opel sedan. Two of my buddies joined me as we explored this beautiful area of low mountains, forests, and hills. Our escapade was short-lived frivolity, however, as we knew the army wasn't about to provide gasoline for such activities. When the gas ran low, we returned the cars to the motor park where we had found them.

It may sound odd and is hard to explain, but the cease-fire had been a real let-down for us. We had been living on adrenaline for months when all of a sudden the war in Europe ended and the necessity for extra adrenaline disappeared. Now we needed some way to adjust to peacetime and normal activity. The Czech car collection gave us a temporary outlet that allowed us to "explode" and then come to grips with what was expected of us.

A hallway 20 feet wide by 300 feet long led to our rooms on the second floor of the dormitory at Kremsmunster. Except for a five-foot-wide walkway, it was absolutely filled with boxes and boxes of loot with labels from all over Europe. While walking to my room the first day, I bumped my foot against the edge of a heavy box. I opened it to see the contents and found eating utensils. I had lost my mess kit sometime back and still needed utensils, so I decided to take a knife and fork.

Once in my room, I looked carefully at the knife and fork and realized that they appeared to be more than just cheap eating utensils. So I dragged the box into my room. In going through it, I found twelve place settings of silver in both luncheon and dinner sizes plus a number of serving pieces. The set was contemporary and very handsome. The silver was new, still in its original packing. On the back of each piece was stamped the number 800 and the Cross of Lorraine. It had a history, I was sure, but by then there was no way to find out what it was.

In one box in the hall there were remnants of cloth, so I took these and wrapped each place setting and serving piece individually. On further searching in the hall, I came upon a bolt of woven cloth with a white-on-white pattern, so I used that to wrap the entire group together. I found a piece of pretty woolen tweed to use as the outside wrap. A local artisan made a sturdy wooden box to hold the wrapped silver. It was ready for mailing.

By this time after war's end, letters could be mailed at will without being censored, but for us to send a package, we were required to have permission signed by an officer. To secure approval to send the silver home, I was told by the lieutenant that I must give him six place settings of the luncheon size silver and some serving pieces. Seeing no alternative, I acquiesced. That still left a full dozen dinner-size place settings, six luncheon-size place settings, plus a number of serving pieces. The silver service now has a history and has been a wonderful conversation piece for my wife and me when we used it for entertaining. We gave the silver service to our daughter, who now enjoys telling the story to their guests.

The first letter I received from my mother after the box arrived barely mentioned the silver but went on and on about the beautiful bolt of satin damask that I had sent. It was the bolt of white "nondescript" cloth that I had used for wrapping the package. A couple of letters later, after researching the silver at the library, she wrote more about it. The Cross of Lorraine stamped on each piece indicated that the silver was of French origin, and the stamped number 800 indicated its silver content; the two stamps signified that it was French sterling silver.

As for the beautiful piece of woolen tweed used to wrap the entire package, I had a tailor make it into a handsome sportcoat that I wore for many years.

19

Waiting to Go Home

In the early weeks after VE Day, confusion reigned throughout the army. There were so many problems in trying to organize an Army of Occupation and in identifying the processes to follow to make it succeed. There had not been a need for anything like this for over two generations, so experience was lacking. The decision from a higher command to transfer eight of us from the 11th Armored Division to an unattached tank battalion—that is, not part of an armored division—after being in Kremsmunster just three weeks was typical of this confusion. And, of all things, the battalion to which we were transferred was quartered in the barracks at Linz from which we had just moved. One of the nice features about Linz was that they had a fine municipal gym where we could take showers. So we moved back and joined the 748th Tank Battalion.

After just two weeks in Linz, the army again transferred the same eight of us, this time to the 68th Tank Battalion, another unattached unit. This battalion was in Austria but was to be moved to a location near Nürnberg, Germany. (Nuremberg is the English spelling of this German city.) The 68th was to become part of the Army of Occupation. General Patton was now the military governor of Bavaria, so approval for the move had to be obtained from him.

Once given the proper clearance from General Patton, we drove the tanks and other vehicles of the 68th Tank Battalion in column

200 miles from Austria to Nürnberg. While awaiting instructions, we camped in a field outside of the city for several days. We were in that field when we unexpectedly received orders to take our tanks and their weapons to a nearby army depot and turn them in. We did that with no regrets. It was a relief to be no longer responsible for a 33-ton monster. We were then transported by truck to the small town of Wassertrudingen, sixty miles southwest of Nürnberg.

At Wassertrudingen, we were assigned to Headquarters Company, 68th Tank Battalion. For the next three months I served in various capacities. My first assignment was as company clerk in Headquarters Company. In this position, I worked closely with the first sergeant. Three weeks after our arrival in Wassertrudingen, however, he was transferred to a unit that was returning to the states. Thus, it became necessary to name another first sergeant. My rank at the time was sergeant (I was wearing three inverted V stripes on each sleeve). There were several sergeants at this rank in the company, but among them, I had the longest time in grade. In the army, time in grade (number of months at the present rank) often determined which person would be advanced to a vacant position. I was not really interested in becoming the first sergeant. However, the sergeant with the time in grade just below mine was a rigid, rank-conscious soldier; most of us thought it would be very difficult to serve under him. So when the position as first sergeant was offered to me, I accepted to protect the men in the company.

I soon found that the officers under whom I was serving were more interested in traveling and roaming around than in paying attention to the duties of the company. Since they were away so much of the time, it fell upon me to assume responsibilities that only a commissioned officer should be taking. After only three weeks as first sergeant, I decided that I was going to get out of that position as soon as something acceptable became available.

Gordon Bickert, a longtime friend who had been in the 11th Armored Division since its inception, was a tank commander and later a platoon sergeant through our combat days. He and I had enjoyed each other's company at chapel and at many events that we had attended in Nürnberg. When we joined the 68th Tank Battalion, he was named battalion sergeant-major, the highest-ranking noncommissioned officer in the battalion. Not long afterward, though,

Bickert's points reached the level where he was eligible to be transferred to a unit returning to the United States.

Lieutenant Kneller, the battalion adjutant in charge of administration of the battalion, had talked to me about taking the position of battalion sergeant-major when Bickert left. When he asked me again, I accepted in order to get away from the job of first sergeant. It was a very interesting job that required lots of paperwork, but it was enjoyable.

It appeared that the role of the American soldier in this Army of Occupation was to make known to the local people that we were in their midst, were carrying weapons, and would use them if the need arose. One small perk was having dinner occasionally in the local hotel, a pleasant relief from GI-prepared food. The German chef served excellent meals and was happy to welcome us any time, since we were paying customers.

This period was an extremely dull time, one of counting the days. Many of us were not happy about being in the army, or about being in Germany, or about being away from home. One night we did have an exciting episode.

The Nazi Party had divided Germany into districts, each one being called a *kreis*. Each *kreis* had a *kreisleiter,* a leader, chosen by the Nazi Party. A headquarters building and a home were provided to the *kreisleiter.* Our offices and living quarters in Wassertrudingen were in the local *kreis* building. The former Nazi *kreisleiter,* named Ittameyer, had disappeared when American troops came to town and had been in hiding since. He had been particularly ruthless in dealing with the local citizenry, so he was not a popular man. In addition, he was on the Nuremberg War Crimes List for having killed two downed Canadian flyers.

The Counter Intelligence Corps (CIC) was a branch of the army whose purpose was to identify any illegal or undercover activity. They had "ears" in many unsuspected places and were answerable only to the highest headquarters of the army.

Receiving word one night that Herr Ittameyer and his wife had secretly come into town and were at the home of his mother-in-law, the Counter Intelligence Corps called and asked me to arrange for four armed guards and a jeep to be ready in ten minutes. Four of us with weapons and a jeep were waiting when the three CIC officers arrived. We headed out to the house of the mother-in-law, where we found the window shutters barred and the heavy outside door closed.

The CIC officer banged on the door. As the mother-in-law answered the door, we raised our weapons. In German, the CIC officer asked, "Is the *kreisleiter* here?" The frightened woman, seeing our guns, answered, "*Jawohl*" (an emphatic "yes, indeed" in German). We quickly moved into the room with weapons poised and there sat Ittameyer, shoes off, almost ready for bed. He and his wife were caught totally by surprise, so they offered no resistance. The CIC officers were very pleased at catching them. They took them to jail in a nearby town to await word from the War Crimes Commission. This was quite a catch for us. Seeing Ittameyer in this setting made me realize that he was a simple peasant who had gone beyond his level of competence by using brute methods. We were all impressed with the Counter Intelligence Corps officers and believed them to be one redeeming feature of the military government.

Several months after the war's end, many of the American soldiers in the Army of Occupation were beginning to recognize increasing restlessness, insolence, and resentment in the German populace. For the first time, many of these people were beginning to realize the consequences of the war they had created. Problems abounded throughout the country but especially so in the cities. There was an inadequate supply of housing because of destruction from air raids and battles and the confiscation of living units for Army of Occupation soldiers. There was a tremendous shortage of food as a result of the lack of normal agricultural production and an inadequate infrastructure to distribute what was available. And last, there was a serious scarcity of all types of heating fuels.

People in cities such as Nürnberg were dying from lack of food and shelter, while the country villages such as Wassertrudingen had a sufficient supply of food and, generally, adequate housing. The only items that most villages lacked were nonessentials such as sugar and cigarettes. The outlook for Germany, and for Europe, was very grim. This was the climate of Germany when I left to attend Biarritz American University in September 1945. Many of us were happy to be leaving.

Sometime before it was clear when the war in Europe would end, plans were made to organize two American-type universities for qualified soldiers, one in England and one in France. These were to offer a wide variety of courses in college-level programs. This was designed to keep the troops occupied while awaiting their return home. For faculty, the army brought in professors who were well-recognized teachers from universities throughout the United States. In France, the American University was developed in Biarritz, a beautiful resort city on the coast of the Bay of Biscay. Biarritz had been Napoleon III's favorite vacation spot where he built a beautiful chateau on the seacoast for his wife, Princess Eugenie. This chateau was subsequently converted into a luxury hotel that joined the other resort hotels along the Atlantic shore. Student soldiers lived at all of those places.

I applied to Biarritz American University for enrollment in the October–December term. After being accepted, I made arrangements to leave my position in Wassertrudingen. There was a large contingent of us going by train from Nürnberg to Paris to Biarritz. We were met at the train station in Biarritz and taken first to one of the beautiful hotels for lunch. We were assigned to hotels of every category throughout the city. A dozen of us were allocated rooms in a small *pensione* within walking distance of the classrooms. Although not fancy, it was superior to anything we had known over the past year. We had still been using our sleeping bags, so having sheets on the bed was a real luxury. Our innkeeper was of Basque extraction, a real character that we all enjoyed. The bonus for our group was that we were assigned to eat our meals at the Miramar Hotel, one of the preeminent seaside resort hotels of Europe. To have delicious meals served to us by French waiters was a new experience.

I chose classes in German, chemistry, and beginning piano. The studies were serious but enjoyable. The classrooms were located in various public buildings throughout the city. Piano lessons were taught at a former school of music arts that was in a villa overlooking the Bay of Biscay. We were also allowed to practice our piano lessons there.

One of my dad's friends was on the faculty teaching forestry, and he invited me to go with his class on a field trip. We were out in a French forest that had been replanted by the French Forest Service. I noticed that the trees had been placed without any particular plan, whereas in Germany, the trees were planted in such orderly fashion that no matter what direction you looked, the trees were growing in a straight line, just like an Iowa cornfield. I commented on this to the French forester accompanying us. His response to me was, "Yes, but in France even the trees like their liberty."

Throughout the school term, we were invited to numerous extracurricular and cultural activities, symphony concerts, drama events, and Christmas programs. The citizens of Biarritz were also invited to these affairs and participated in large numbers. Having been with no one but soldiers for months and months, we thoroughly enjoyed the privilege of being with men and women who were wearing civilian clothes rather than uniforms.

Even in a resort city such as Biarritz, the deprivations of war were still in evidence. We student soldiers became very involved in the welfare of the Biarritz community and its citizens. We organized and collected several large funds. One was to provide gifts for local children who otherwise would have no Christmas. Medical care for many of the children was lacking, so another fund went to support that. The third fund was dedicated to aiding the needy regardless of age. That was our thanks to a Biarritz that had been extremely hospitable to us.

The town of Lourdes was where Bernadette had a number of visions in which she saw the Virgin Mother at the Grotto. The army made arrangements for interested soldiers to visit there. One Friday, a special car was attached to the regular train from Biarritz to Lourdes, and a group of us filled the car. It was a four-hour ride up in the Pyrenees Mountains. The stories of Bernadette and the Grotto were very interesting. The first night there, one of the boys in our six-bed room teased two daughters of the innkeeper at supper. So after the lights were out and we had gone to bed, all of a sudden we were drenched with buckets of cold water. We had a water fight, but after getting the best of us, the girls left. I guess we were still adolescents; it added to the fun of the trip. We returned on Sunday to be ready for classes on Monday.

On a cold rainy Saturday in early December, several of us took the fifteen-minute train ride to St. Jean de Luz, a typical Basque fishing village on the Bay of Biscay, adjacent to Spain. From there we took a cog railway to the top of a nearby mountain peak. After we reached the top, we climbed a barbed-wire fence and walked over into Spain. This was a major offense if caught, as Spain was off-limits to all American soldiers. Before we went up the mountain, we had left two boxes of 10-in-1 rations at a local restaurant. When we came down several hours later, we went to the restaurant and ate dinner. The French definitely knew what to do to convert raw materials into delicious meals.

On a visit to the battalion doctor back in Wassertrudingen, I had been told that frostbite of my feet during the Battle of the Bulge had caused changes in the blood vessels and tissues. The doctor said that my feet would become somewhat less sensitive with time, but from now on, I would always be bothered by cold weather. We had a cold spell in December in Biarritz, and I was having trouble keeping my feet warm, so I had been wearing the felt boots that my folks sent to me in Belgium. After being out in the cold most of one day, my feet were really bothering me. When I arrived back at the *pensione,* I found that there was no heat in our rooms because of the fuel shortage all over Europe. The only heat available was the hot water in the plumbing fixtures, so I filled the bidet in my room with water as hot as I could tolerate and soaked my feet for several hours. I repeated that process a number of times in the next few days and was very grateful for that piece of plumbing.

During that term, the army officials decided to close Biarritz American University. It had served its purpose. Many soldiers had already returned to the United States, decreasing the number of troops still in Europe. The soldiers who remained were needed to man the Army of Occupation in Germany. Classes at Biarritz ended two days before Christmas. We had very meaningful church services and parties for the local people. Christmas dinner at the Miramar Hotel was a sumptuous feast. When I got back to the *pensione,* the innkeeper was waiting for me. He had noticed that I didn't care for wine, so he insisted that I come into his living room and have a small glass of a French liqueur. In handing it to me, he said, "Water is for fish, alcohol is for people." I accepted his hospitality.

During the last weeks in Biarritz, I had lost communication with the 68th Tank Battalion and, despite several telephone calls, had not been able to find where they were. One small piece of information suggested that the battalion might be at Reims, France, preparing to return to the United States. So on December 26th, I caught the train to Paris and changed to a train going to Reims, where I was able to get a bed at the army billet. The next morning, I went to the army headquarters to find out more about the 68th Tank Battalion. I discovered that it had already sailed from France. I also learned that I was assigned to Headquarters Company of the 70th Tank Battalion, which was in Nürnberg. While in Reims, I had the opportunity to visit the little schoolhouse near the railroad tracks where the Germans had signed the unconditional surrender that would be effective on May 8, 1945. The walls of this room had the maps showing the location of all Allied troops on VE Day. One map showed the 11th Armored Division to be farthest east of all Allied troops in Europe. That did not surprise me, but it was nice to see it documented.

That day I caught the train back to Paris, where I was able to get reservations on a very nice prewar train to Nürnberg. A waiter came through and called us to the diner shortly after we pulled out of the station. It was an enjoyable, leisurely meal. The reclining seats in the coach were very comfortable, so I had a good night's sleep. I awoke the next morning in time to see us crossing the Rhine River not far from where we had crossed it on a pontoon bridge one year earlier.

When I reached Nürnberg, I called Headquarters Company of the 70th Tank Battalion, which was stationed there. They had been expecting me and sent a car to pick me up and take me to their quarters, which were housed in German government apartments. I was assigned to share a one-room apartment with a soldier named Stephens. There was no central heating, so we had to keep the place warm by burning wood in a stove placed in the center of the room. We had cleaning service and laundry done by local German women for a small sum of money each month.

When I returned to Germany in late December, I was surprised to encounter a country that seemed much better off than when I had left. The attitude of the German people seemed markedly improved. The occupation looked as though it was functioning effectively. The United States had sent large amounts of foods and grains for all of Europe, including Germany. They seemed surprised but appreciative that we were bringing in food for them. Hope was in the air.

I was to spend the next two months awaiting my return home. With no specific duties, Steve and I were able to go swimming at an enclosed city pool, go to sporting events, and attend dramatic and musical productions at the Nürnberg Opera House, which, miraculously enough, suffered only modest damage from the air raids and battles. The streetcars were back in full operation and provided great transportation that was free to American soldiers. We could see that it had been a beautiful city before war's devastation. In our travels about, we realized that at least twenty-five square miles of the city were in shambles.

It was during this period that I had the opportunity to attend the Nuremberg War Crimes Trials. The formal name for this was the International Military Tribunal of Nuremberg. Its purpose was to provide a civil trial for German leaders who had committed major war crimes. The men on trial at this time were fifteen of the major Nazi leaders. Others, including Hitler, would have been tried but were no longer living. The trial was held at the original German Palace of Justice on the east side of the city. The army had reconstructed all of the war-damaged areas of the main building and its connecting prison buildings. It was an impressive site for such judicial activities.

My roommate and I were required to set up an appointment for the date we wished to attend a session of the trials. On that date, we entered the Palace of Justice, where we were processed through a well-designed security system. We were given tickets for admission to the courtroom. The court was in recess when we arrived, so we stood in the corridor awaiting its resumption. While we were waiting, three of the prisoners—Wilhelm Keitel, Albert Speers, and Rudolph Hess—walked past, one at a time. Hess, doing a German-army goosestep, looked like a sick man, pale and unhealthy.

As the trial resumed, we entered the balcony and took a seat. The fifteen defendants were all in their assigned chairs with the exception of Arthur Seyss-Inquart. No explanation was given for his absence. Hermann Goering sat slumped in his chair, resting his head on his right hand most of the time and appearing completely disinterested. Hess, not wearing his earphones, also appeared disinterested. Of all the defendants, Hjalmar Schacht appeared to be paying the most attention.

Every person in the courtroom was given earphones that had five channels to choose from. Channel One broadcast the voice of the person speaking at the time, while the other four channels gave simultaneous translation into English, Russian, French, and German.

The French were presenting evidence from Alsace-Lorraine and from the Battle of the Bulge at Malmedy and St. Vith in Belgium. We felt very privileged to have been allowed to visit the trials on this interesting day. No judicial decisions would be made until many months later after all of the evidence had been presented to the presiding judges representing the United States, England, France, and Russia. Once the decision and judgment on these leading persons was made, the tribunal would consider others on its War Crimes List.

In early February, six weeks after returning to Nürnberg, I received orders to enter the pipeline for return to the United States and discharge from the army. Upon the assigned date, several truckloads of soldiers from various parts of Germany arrived at the train station in Augsburg and were driven out to the freight yards. There awaiting us was an entire train of "40 and 8" freight cars. These were small French freight cars so named in World War I because they could haul either forty men or eight horses. From the looks and the smell, our car had been hauling horses.

Our 40 and 8 car was even "winterized." In it sat a small coal-burning stove and three tiny bags of coal. However, there was no chimney to create a draft to draw the smoke. Several of us went out to find and "requisition" two sections of stovepipe and an elbow while the remaining men swept out the car. We found two stove-pipes and an ell and connected them, only to find that there was no hole in the wall or door to pass the pipe through. We definitely needed the heat, so the only option available was to keep the sliding door slightly open even though it was February in a cold winter.

Never mind, we were going home. Nothing else really mattered.

Since we were in freight cars, we were connected to engines that only pulled slow freight trains. There were no eating facilities on the train, so it periodically stopped at transient army messes run by several U.S. soldiers and some German prisoners of war. The first mess we stopped at served us fried chicken for breakfast. When we stopped for lunch, we were served hot soup made from canned sausage. It was inedible. Fortunately, we had two cases of K-rations in our freight car, so did have something to eat. The next morning we had an excellent hot breakfast.

When we arrived in France, our train was attached to French-rail-system engines, and we really began to move. At one stop they

French "40 and 8" freight cars carry soldiers headed for the United States and discharge. U.S. Army, *Thunderbolts in the ETO.*

told us that we would be there for an hour, so we went off in search of a bakery to get some French baguettes. A Frenchman from the train went with us to help. We were unsuccessful, as the only thing the bakery had was the dough being mixed for the following morning. We started back to the train and met one of the trainmen looking for us. The Frenchman who had accompanied us was the fireman for our train, and it was ready to go. Thank goodness they had held the train for the fireman. The next transient mess where we stopped served a breakfast of turkey, peas, and potatoes. Few of us ate there.

Never mind, we were going home.

After three days in frigid 40 and 8 freight cars, we finally pulled into Le Havre, France. Army trucks met us and took us to Camp Philip Morris, the army port from which we would board a ship to return home. We settled into our tent by 1:30 P.M., but no provision had been made to feed us lunch. The next meal would be served at 6 P.M. We had no way to clean up, as water was not scheduled to come on in our latrine until 5 P.M. It actually did come on then.

Never mind, we were going home.

Camp Philip Morris was slithering in mud from recent rains. Some tents had electric lights in them, but not ours. There was one potbellied stove in our fifteen-by-thirty-foot tent to keep forty men warm. We learned that there were Red Cross clubs on base, but none were near us and no transportation was available. They had ice cream for sale, provided you had francs. Of course, we had no francs.

Never mind, we were going home.

We found the water on in the latrine the next morning, so we took showers. The warm (not hot) water ran out halfway through, so we finished with a cold shower. The weather was cold and damp there, especially at night. Some soldiers we met had more points than we had and were still waiting for their ship. That caused us some concern.

We were at Camp Philip Morris for eight days. Some things improved. We were able to exchange some money for French francs, so we could purchase ice cream at the Red Cross. Dinner the last night consisted of cold canned tomatoes with chopped onions for

Home at last, March 1946. Hartman gets a hug from his mother.

the main course. Bread and jam were included. Dessert was crushed pineapple.

Never mind, we were going home.

On March 2, 1946, we boarded our ship, the *New Bern Victory,* where we found our bunks in the hold. It was a large area fitted with steel-framed bunks stacked four high. The foundation of the bunk was a piece of canvas lashed to a steel frame with rope. We slept in or on our sleeping bags. The sleeping arrangement was adequate. Ventilation down there was okay, especially compared with the ventilation in the HMT *Samaria.* This hold did not smell like the locker room in a high school gym. The food was fairly good. The weather was gorgeous on the voyage home, so we sat and lay around the deck talking and reading. It was a very restful eight days.

After disembarking in New York, we were transferred to trains for travel to the discharge center nearest our home. I was sent to the center at Camp Grant near Rockford, Illinois. On March 14, 1946, I received my discharge and took the train to Chicago, where I changed to the Chicago and Northwestern Railroad and caught the train to Ames, Iowa.

My dad and brother-in-law met me at the station when the train arrived in Ames at 3 o'clock on the morning of March 15, 1946. After almost three years filled with incredible experiences, I was home.

20

Belgium Remembers: Fiftieth Anniversary of the Battle of the Bulge

The ceremony commemorating the fiftieth anniversary of the beginning of the Battle of the Bulge was to be held on December 16, 1994, in Bastogne, Belgium. My wife and I were invited to attend by Docteur Jean Lewalle, a friend we had met at several international orthopaedic surgery meetings. He and his wife Nicole hosted our visit, and we stayed with them at their home outside Brussels. Jean was 14 years old and living in Liege, Belgium, during the World War II battles.

We went with the Lewalles to Bastogne several days before the ceremonies were to take place. There we met two of their closest friends, André Burnotte and his wife, Monique. André was 13, living in Chenogne, near Bastogne, when the 11th Armored Division battled for that village.

Lieutenant Colonel Emile Engel, a Belgian Army historian and expert on the Battle of the Bulge, interpreted for us as the Burnottes drove us through some of the areas where my company had fought.

In the village of Bercheux where we had returned several times for rest and to repair our tanks, I recognized a house where some of us had stayed with a Belgian family. We knocked on the door, and the woman who answered was Marguerite, the daughter of the family, who was 19 when we stayed there. She invited us in and

Hosts for Jean and Ted Hartman's return to Belgium for the December 1994 fiftieth anniversary of the Battle of the Bulge. *Back row, left to right:* Monique Burnotte, André Burnotte, Nicole Lewalle. *Front row, left to right:* Françoise Neven (deceased), Ted Hartman, Jean Hartman, and Jean Lewalle.

The Hartmans and hosts are greeted by Marguerite Fortemaison at her home in Bercheux, Belgium, where soldiers (including Hartman) stayed in 1944.

called her sister, Anna, on the telephone and we talked briefly with Colonel Engel interpreting.

Leaving Bercheux, we went to Sibret, Morhet, and on to Houmont. These villages were all in the path of our first vicious fighting. I recognized much of the terrain as we drove through the fields and ended up on a hill that overlooked Chenogne. It was here that the Germans shelled us so mercilessly on New Year's Eve, 1944, as we poured gasoline into our tanks. The next day, New Year's Day, we took the town from the Germans. Twenty-nine out of thirty-one homes and the village church had been destroyed during the battles. Today, Chenogne is a lovely pastoral village that has been completely rebuilt.

The weather had become quite cold and was intermittently raining and sleeting, reminiscent of December 1944. We proceeded to Noville, where we saw the rebuilt church and the crossroads from which a German antitank gun had hit one of our company's tanks, disabling it and blocking our path for retreat. In 1945, the road was barely wide enough for one tank to pass; today it is a three-lane highway.

We found the remains of the apple orchard where we had coiled while we made plans to get back to our own lines. In 1945, our tank had dropped into the foundation of a burned-out house. Fifty years later, a house had been built on the foundation. The hedgerow in front of the house was familiar, and from there we could see the route that we had followed through the deep snow from Noville.

At Foy, we went to a cemetery for the German soldiers killed in battles in this area. It was very dark and bleak. There were many dark-gray marble crosses with three names on each side, presumably meaning six bodies in each grave. Many of them were only 15 and 16 years old.

That evening, the Burnottes took us to their lovely home in the country outside Liege, where we had dinner with their family and spent the night. The next morning, we returned to Chenogne with André and Monique and attended a memorable Mass in the rebuilt church. After the service, a ceremony was held to dedicate a memorial to the citizens of Chenogne who died in the fighting in 1944 and 1945, one of whom was André Burnotte's aunt. During this ceremony, the mayor, speaking in French, began telling some of my war

Ted Hartman is presented with honorary citizenship of Chenogne, Belgium, by Mayor Michelle Detaille on December 11, 1994.

history and how honored the village was to have me return. After the "Star Spangled Banner" and "la Brabanconne" (the Belgian National Anthem) were played, the entire group moved to the village school, where I was made an honorary citizen of Chenogne. This was quite an emotional experience for me. I was also given a beautiful pewter dish with the seal of the district on it and a book about the Luxembourg District of Belgium. Many of the local citizens had signed it and written messages. I was asked to relate my recollection of the battle for Chenogne. They seemed very interested in hearing this. Colonel Engel interpreted.

Several days later, Jean Lewalle took us to Liege, his hometown. We went to the American Cemetery at Henri Chapelle. It was strikingly beautiful, light and airy. The crosses and Stars of David marked the graves lined in neat rows when viewed from any direction. This was in sharp contrast to the German cemetery at Foy. Many of the soldiers killed in the Battle of the Bulge were buried here. A computerized record of the location of every soldier buried in an American cemetery is maintained at all American cemetery offices. I asked at the office about the location of my buddies who

The Mardasson, a stunning star-shaped memorial built at Bastogne by a grateful Belgian nation, is dedicated to the enduring friendship of the people of Belgium and the United States. The 50th-anniversary memorial service in memory of those men killed in the Battle of the Bulge was held here.

were killed in the Battle of the Bulge. I was told that the remains of many had been returned to the United States. Of those still in Europe, all but one was buried in the Luxembourg American Cemetery at Hamm, Luxembourg. At the cemetery in Henri Chapelle, we learned that many Belgian families have adopted the graves of American soldiers. They tend the graves and bring flowers on any special day of commemoration.

Later that week, we returned to Bastogne to participate in the ceremonies marking the fiftieth anniversary of the start of the Battle of the Bulge. We stayed at the home of Françoise Neven, a friend of the Lewalles. During dinner that evening, we could hear the guns practicing for the following day's ceremonies.

On the morning of December 16th, we awoke to cold and snowy weather, much like it had been exactly fifty years ago to the day. Similar weather had not occurred on that date in any of the intervening years. We dressed warmly and went to the church for the start of the ceremonies. The church was filled with veterans of the Battle of the Bulge and their families who had returned for this meaningful event. Mass was conducted by the Bishop of Bastogne and a Catholic priest from Providence, Rhode Island, who had been a combat soldier in the Battle of the Bulge. It was a beautiful service. At its conclusion, we were taken to the Mardasson, a handsome star-shaped memorial to the American soldiers killed in the Battle of the Bulge. We had seats under awnings and were provided with wool blankets to keep warm.

The King of Belgium, U.S. Ambassador to the United Nations Madeleine Albright, the commanding general of the American Forces in Europe, and other dignitaries entered. Once they were seated, wreaths were presented, the national anthems of Belgium and the United States were played, and several speeches were given. The ceremony was closed by a touching rendition of taps performed with an echo. It was a moving ceremony.

Next, those present went to the General Patton Memorial. Schoolchildren joined us here, and each child took the hand of a veteran. Two cute sixth-grade boys took our hands, and we marched with them several blocks to McAuliffe Square, named after the American general who refused to surrender Bastogne to the Germans. A Sherman tank stands on a pedestal in the square.

Afterward, we went to the city hall. From the balcony we watched a dramatic reenactment of the Battle of the Bulge on the street below. The pageant included people fleeing from the Germans in horse-drawn carts, a simulated air raid and bombing, the first arrival of American troops and tanks followed by their retreat, and then the final return of the Americans.

The next morning, André Burnotte took us to the caserne, an army barracks, where a number of privately owned tanks were on display. I had the opportunity to climb onto a Sherman tank and to stand in the commander's hatch in the turret. When they drove off in a big roar, I was reminded anew of how terribly noisy they were.

We returned to Chenogne to visit the Burnotte family farm. André showed us the field where his mother had taken him, four siblings, and six cousins to lay in the snow for four hours during the height of the battle for Chenogne.

We saw the family home and the beautiful little chapel that their father had rebuilt after the previous one was destroyed during the

Sherman tank recovered from a battlefield near Bastogne, Belgium, was used in the 1994 re-enactment of the Battle of Bastogne. Ted Hartman stands in the tank commander's hatch.

fighting. They showed us a tree by the roadside that had a large hole cut in it. The German plan had been to place an explosive in the hole, blow up the tree, and block the road. However, they were driven out of town before the explosive could be put in place.

This return visit to Belgium was memorable. Seeing the battlefields where we fought was fascinating and at times emotional for me. Meeting and getting to know a number of the Belgian people in their own setting was most rewarding. They are a people forever grateful to the United States for bringing them their freedom, as we were told many times. It was a wonderful experience.

21

Belgium Revisited, May 2000:
Belgian Memorial Day

A Sherman tank has rested on a pedestal in McAuliffe Square in Bastogne for more than fifty years. Because the 4th Armored Division was the first unit to open a road into the encircled city of Bastogne, it was assumed by the local Belgian authorities that this tank was from one of the battalions of the 4th. Recently, historians from the Cercle d'Histoire de Bastogne studied the location of the field from which the tank was recovered and found that the only American division that had been in battle in that particular area was the 11th Armored. A ceremony was planned for Belgian Memorial Day, May 30, 2000, to dedicate the tank to its correct identity. I decided to go to Bastogne for the event.

I arrived in the Bastogne area several days before the ceremony and visited some of the sites that were meaningful from my battle experiences in 1944 and 1945. I photographed these places as they appeared fifty-five years later and recalled some of the events that had occurred there. These recollections follow.

Our battalion bivouacked in a field near Longlier, Belgium, the night prior to entry into battle. Fifty-five years later, I easily recognized the field beside the highway to Bastogne. I remembered the night before combat. We had performed maintenance on our tanks and had eaten a cold supper of C-rations (canned beans). Following that, we rolled our sleeping bags out on the snow-covered ground. Between the cold and thinking about entry into battle the next day, sleep did not come easily. Our initial combat experiences the following day would be the real test. How would we respond?

Then I proceeded along our route north toward the point of entry into battle. First came Bercheux, the village where we returned for maintenance and rest between combat assignments. In the center of town, on the highway, was the home where we stayed with a Belgian family. They had been very hospitable even though crowded when ten American soldiers moved in with them. I remembered the daughter making hot chocolate for us each evening. Several of the older men in our group had played poker in the living room at every opportunity. This town had become a safe haven for us.

Leaving Bercheux, I drove toward Bastogne, turned north off the main highway, and went through Morhet and on to Lavaselle, our objective for that first day in battle. Along this road, I came upon the fields where we had entered combat. Seeing these fields reminded me of the fear of the reality of battle. At the time, we wondered what it would be like and how we would perform. Had we been adequately trained? In retrospect, I realized how valuable our training and maneuver experiences had been at Camp Cooke and also in England. Although not the real thing, it was similar enough to allow us to perform our duties by rote. I noticed the forests that lay alongside the fields and thought of our concern those many years ago that they were providing a perfect defense cover for enemy soldiers and antitank guns.

I still have a mind's-eye picture of watching through the periscope that first morning when all of our tanks seemed to be going in different directions. Yet on that first day in battle, we gained our objective. At the end of the day, we also learned that a number of our tanks were missing. The sad realization that some of my friends were in those tanks flooded my thoughts once again.

Moving on, I stood on the hill that looked down into Chenogne. I was reminded of how the Germans bombarded us with incendiary shells just as we were pouring gasoline into our tanks. They really gave us a New Year's welcome complete with a fireworks display. Seeing a completely rebuilt peaceful Chenogne, I remembered the almost total destruction of the village and its church. Today Belgian and American flags fly over the memorial that was dedicated to those citizens of Chenogne who died in the 1944/45 battles.

Driving on north, I saw the road sign to Mande St. Etienne, which brought back a very vivid memory. An 18-year-old soldier in our company was standing in front of our tank when some German rockets landed. As I watched through the periscope, the explosion lifted this young man straight up in the air and then laid him back on the ground, motionless. A devastating sight. His young widowed wife was expecting a baby. Again, how very sad.

A tremendous artillery barrage followed by our tank and infantry advance devastated Mande St. Etienne. I recalled the spooky light from burning buildings that hung over the town. How glad we were the following morning to be relieved from the front line by the 17th Airborne Division. And what a good feeling it was to move to Bercheux for nine days of respite from the intensity of battle.

In 1944/45, we did not know that our first encounter with the enemy was with troops from the Führer Begleit Brigade. This unit was personally controlled by Hitler through Colonel Otto Ernst Remer. Colonel Remer had been with Hitler when the attempt was made to assassinate him and had identified the guilty parties, thus becoming one of Hitler's most favored commanders.

The Führer Begleit Brigade was comprised of highly trained and skilled soldiers who were regarded as Germany's best. That was who we met in our first battle encounter. In retrospect, it is no surprise that we lost so many tanks and had such heavy casualties in those early days of combat. Other German fighting units that we met during that period were the Panzer Lehr Division and the 26th Volksgrenadier Division, both highly respected, almost professional organizations. They were deadly enemies.

I remembered how cold it was inside that tank with frost on the interior walls. Not only were tanks cold because of the below-freezing temperatures, but the rear-mounted engine drew the air needed for its operation through the tank from vents in the front. In Belgium in January, that was frigid air.

Fifty-five years later, the approach to Noville from the south looked familiar. I could "see" our infantry riding in several half-tracks when they were struck by enemy fire. The view of one soldier trapped in a burning half-track, a devastating sight, is still clear in my mind to this day. Moving toward Noville, I stopped the car and walked into the field through which we had approached that village. The forests that had lined the field on the east were no longer there. I kept thinking how much easier the battle for Noville would have been without the cover of those woods where the enemy was dug in and directing fire on us.

Driving on into Noville, I was very conscious of the fact that the main road through town was now a three-lane highway, whereas in 1945, it was barely wide enough for one tank to pass. I stood in the apple orchard where we coiled in a large circle to protect each other's backside. Looking back toward the church, I could still visualize German soldiers in those ugly helmets coming toward us with bazookas.

A house has been built on the sunken foundation that our tank dropped into during the ambush in Noville. Standing in front of that house, I saw the hedgerow that we hid beside, then the valley we followed and the creek that we crossed to reach our own lines, all in deep snow. We did not know the password for the day. Would the American soldiers shoot or would they ask us to advance and be recognized? As it turned out, they had been informed that we might be coming and would not know the password and were to be allowed to pass through.

I noticed a barn in Foy that looked like the building where the battalion aid station was set up and where we took Baudouin to receive care for his burned eyes. How relieved I was when I saw Sergeant Ammons there in 1945.

It was outside Foy that I reflected on the changes in leadership that B Company had experienced so quickly in the early days of combat. When Captain Ameno, our original company commander, was killed on the first day in battle, Lieutenant Williamson took command. Four days later, as we were approaching Mande St. Etienne, Lieutenant Williamson was hit in the head by shrapnel, necessitating his evacuation. The next officer in rank took command and led us into the ambush at Noville, after which both he and the ranking second lieutenant went to the medics and were evacuated to the rear. At that point, one officer remained in our company. We were fearful of his leadership, as he was quite immature and reckless. We were all relieved when Lieutenant Grayson was assigned to take command of B Company. He had been in command of the battalion assault guns and was an extremely able, highly respected commander.

Last, I went to Binsfeld, Luxembourg, and found the area to be as fertile and lush as I recalled. I went up a hill to a field at the edge of town where we had a motor park for the tanks. While looking at the field, I remembered very clearly how several of us began playing cowboys and Indians one afternoon just as we completed work. One of our submachine guns fired unexpectedly. No one was injured, but it frightened us and sobered us very quickly.

On the day before the dedication, I returned to Bastogne with my friend, Jean Lewalle. We went to McAuliffe Square, where the tank rests on its pedestal. The Cercle d'Histoire de Bastogne had identified the tank to be one named Barracuda from Company B, 41st Tank Battalion, 11th Armored Division. The historians were able to locate one of the original crew members, Ivan Goldstein, who then visited Bastogne and confirmed that the tank was indeed Barracuda, in which he had served as the assistant driver. One of the confirming pieces of information was material that was splattered all over the interior wall of the turret. Ivan Goldstein had bought a carton of chewing gum before leaving England and stored it in a cache in the turret. In studying that material, it was determined that it was the residual of exploded gum. When I learned that Ivan would be attending the rededication, I decided to attend.

Ivan Goldstein and I had been good friends in the Army ASTP program at the University of Oregon. When the army discontinued the program, Goldstein and I were both assigned to Company B, 41st Tank Battalion, 11th Armored Division, where the friendship continued. We had lost contact over the ensuing years.

At McAuliffe Square we met Helen Urda, widow of the driver of Barracuda, and her children, Greg and Alene. Soon, a couple came walking across the square toward us. It was Ivan Goldstein and his wife, June. Here we were, together again after more than fifty years.

Hosting that day's events and the rededication of Barracuda in McAuliffe Square were Robert Fergloute and Roger Marquet of the Cercle d'Histoire de Bastogne. After greeting each other, we rode in jeeps of World War II vintage to the nearby village of Tillet. In taking this village from the Germans in 1945, one company from the 55th Armored Infantry Battalion of the 11th Armored Division lost forty men killed of the 200 in the company.

More than 100 people gathered for the special ceremony that dedicated a memorial plaque to the lives of those men. Seeing the local schoolchildren, whose teachers had brought them to participate in this ceremony, really impressed me. I suspect the Belgian people and their children are more aware of the participation of the United States in World War II and its significance than are the younger generations of Americans. The national anthems of the United States and Belgium were played to conclude the program.

We rode in the jeeps to the starting point of battle action by Company B. On that first day of battle, one part of the column of B Company vehicles turned off toward Morhet and the other went north to Sibret. Both columns would eventually come back together at the objective, Lavaselle.

Driving to Lavaselle and then Renuamont, we came upon the field between Hubermont and Renuamont from which the tank Barracuda had been removed in September 1948 to be placed in McAuliffe Square in Bastogne. Historians told us that on December 30, 1944, a local resident, Mr. Edouard Reisen, was watching from a window in his home when he saw an American tank enter the south side of this field. Although not knowing that the command staff of the Führer Begleit Brigade was located there, the tank moved almost to the top of Renuamont Hill, then completely reversed direction and headed back downhill.

As the tank came back toward the Reisen home, it bogged down in an unrecognized marsh which was covered by deep snow and ice. Unable to move, the tank became a sitting target for enemy weapons. It is believed that a *panzerfaust* hit the rear of the American tank first but did not disable it, as the tank continued to try to move from the marsh. As Mr. Reisen watched, a German panther tank came from Renuamont, stopped beside his house, and fired a projectile that hit Barracuda on its left side, setting fire to the inside of the tank.

Mr. Reisen saw the crew abandon the burning tank. The commander of the tank, Wallace Alexander, sustained serious injuries to both legs but somehow got out of the tank to lie in the snow. Of the two other members of the turret crew, Cecil Peterman sustained a

Ivan Goldstein stands in the doorway of the pigsty at the Lhoas farm, Hubermont, Belgium, where he and Andrew Urda were held prisoners.

major injury to the back of his chest and lay face down in the snow with his wounds exposed. The story of the third member of the turret crew, Dage Hebert, is not fully known. Alexander and Peterman were cared for by German medics and both became prisoners of war.

With water coming up into the bottom of the tank, driver Andrew Urda and assistant driver Ivan Goldstein climbed out through a turret hatch and jumped from the tank into the snow. Both sank to their necks in icy water. Thinking this would be a good place to hide, they stayed immersed as long as possible. As soon as they surfaced, however, they were faced by German soldiers with weapons trained on them and were ordered out of the water. The two were ordered to carry Alexander, the wounded tank commander, to the German medical aid station up the hill toward the neighboring Lhoas farm. There the German medics completed the amputation of one of Alexander's legs. Although Urda and Goldstein lost track of Alexander, they learned after the war that he died soon thereafter from complications of his injuries.

After that, Urda and Goldstein were marched to the German

command post beyond the aid station in the nearby Lhoas home. They were imprisoned in a pigsty at the farm with several other American soldiers from the 101st Airborne Division. Urda and Goldstein were separately taken to the adjacent farmhouse, where they were interrogated by a German major who had lived in the United States and who spoke excellent English. The major first interrogated Urda, became convinced that he was Jewish (even though his dog tag identified his religion as Byzantine Catholic), and ordered him to be shot at daybreak the following morning. Goldstein was next brought before the major, who looked at his dog tag that identified his religion as H, for Hebrew. He also found a letter in Goldstein's pocket from his mother reminding him not to forget to celebrate an upcoming Jewish holiday. With that, the major became angry and ordered him also returned to the pigsty to be shot at daybreak the following day.

As fortune would have it, the 11th Armored Division began battle before sunrise, December 31st, with an intense artillery barrage. Part of this barrage was aimed at the Lhoas farmhouse and barn where the German field headquarters was located. The pigsty where Goldstein and Urda were imprisoned was in a separate building a short distance from the house. The barn and house caught fire from the shelling, forcing the Germans to evacuate the farm and flee. The pigsty was not damaged.

Under guard of a German soldier, the American prisoners were marched in the freezing cold wind and snow fifty miles to Prum, Germany, without eating or drinking. A German guard, seeing that Goldstein's boots were in better condition than his own, forced him at gunpoint to take off his boots and give them to him. This left Goldstein barefoot while hiking in the snow and ice. Following this, Urda and Goldstein were identified only as prisoners of war, so religion played no further role during their captivity.

The full story of Goldstein and Urda as prisoners of war tells of unbelievably inhumane treatment while they served as slave laborers and were moved deeper and deeper into Germany to escape the advancing American army. They were near death in Stalag XII A at Limburg, Germany, when they were freed by American troops in April 1945. At that time, both had contracted diphtheria in addition to suffering from severe malnutrition. Ivan Goldstein was tall and

Greg Urda, Ivan Goldstein, and Ted Hartman stand on the left side of Barracuda, the Sherman tank that stands on a pedestal in McAuliffe Square, Bastogne. Recently identified as Barracuda, from Company B, 41st Tank Battalion, 11th Armored Division, by researchers from the Cercle d'Histoire de Bastogne. Note the hole behind the 11th Armored Division insignia made by a German armor-piercing projectile.

Barracuda from behind. Note the defect caused by a projectile from a German bazooka.

weighed 205 pounds when he was captured. When he was freed four months later, he weighed 95 pounds. Urda and Goldstein both required long periods of intensive medical care before they recovered.

On Belgian Memorial Day, May 30, 2000, a crowd gathered in McAuliffe Square for the rededication of the tank to its true identity, Barracuda, Company B, 41st Tank Battalion, 11th Armored Division. The program for the ceremony included brief words from the mayor of Bastogne and from officials of the Cercle d'Histoire de Bastogne. Helen Urda and her son, Greg, unveiled the new plaque identifying the tank's origin. It was a very touching ceremony which ended with the playing of the national anthems of both countries. Following this, a reception was held in the Maison de Ville (city hall), at which the veterans of the Battle of the Bulge in attendance were presented with the Medal of Freedom of Bastogne, a highly treasured recognition.

This return to Belgium brought back many memories. May we never again see such a vicious and cataclysmic series of events such as the ones that almost destroyed the world during World War II.

BIBLIOGRAPHY

Books and Pamphlets

Cole, Hugh M. 1965. *The Ardennes: The Battle of the Bulge.* Washington, D.C.: Office of the Chief of Military History, Department of the Army.

Cooper, Belton Y. 1998. *Death Traps: The Survival of an American Armored Division in World War II.* Novato, Calif.: Presidio Press.

Degive, Jacques, Robert Fergloute, and Roger Marquet. 1999. *The "Sherman" at McAuliffe Square in Bastogne.* Bastogne: Cercle d'Histoire de Bastogne.

Dupuy, Trevor N., David L. Bongard, and Richard C. Anderson. 1994. *Hitler's Last Gamble: The Battle of the Bulge, December 1944–January 1945.* New York: Harper Perennial.

Farago, Ladislas. 1965. *Patton: Ordeal and Triumph.* New York: Dell Publishing Company.

Keough, Emmett L. 1944. *Thunderbolt Eleventh Armored Division: A Natural.* Camp Cooke, Calif.: Eleventh Armored Division Public Relations Office.

Knight, Robert B. 1945. *Battalion War History, Forty-first Tank Battalion.* Army pamphlet distributed to 11th Armored Division in Austria. N.p.

MacDonald, Charles B. 1985. *A Time for Trumpets: The Untold Story of the Battle of the Bulge.* New York: William Morrow.

Parker, Danny S. 1991. *Battle of the Bulge: Hitler's Ardennes Offensive, 1944–1945.* Philadelphia: Combined Books.

Patton, George S., Jr. 1947. *War As I Knew It.* Boston: Houghton Mifflin Company.

Persico, Joseph E. 1995. *Nuremburg: Infamy on Trial.* New York: Penguin Books.

Steward, Hal D. 1948. *Thunderbolt.* Washington, D.C.: 11th Armored Division Association.

U.S. Army. 1945. *The Story of the Eleventh Armored Division.* Army pamphlet distributed to the 11th Armored Division in Austria. N.p.

———. 1945. *Thunderbolts in the ETO.* 1945. Army pamphlet distributed to the 11th Armored Division in Austria. N.p.

Zaher, William J. 1945. *Company B, Forty-first Tank Battalion War Diary.* Bad Hall, Austria: G. Mittermoller.

Internet References

Bundesministerium für Inneres (Austria). "The Mauthausen Concentration Camp 1938–1945." Available online at: http://www.mauthausen-memorial.gv.at/engl/einstieg.html

Châtel, Vincent, and Chuck Ferree. "The Forgotten Camps: Mauthausen." Available online at: http://www.jewishgen.org/ForgottenCamps/Camps/MauthausenEng.html

Dickinson, Kendra. "Mauthausen Concentration Camp." Available online at: http://www.geocities.com/the11thada/history/mauthausen/mauthausen_camp.htm

Van Dyke, Wayne. "Battle of the Bulge: The Communique." Available online at: http://www.users.skynet.be/bulgecriba/vandyke.html

Letters

Hartman, J. Ted. 1943–1946. Letters to Mr. and Mrs. George B. Hartman, Ames, Iowa from various army locations.

Interviews

Goldstein, Ivan. 2001. Interview with the author. Kalamazoo, Michigan.

INDEX

Page references in italics indicate information contained in maps, photographs, or illustrations.

J. Ted Hartman was 19 years old when he drove a tank into combat during the Battle of the Bulge. After receiving a discharge from the army, he enrolled in pre-medical studies at Iowa State College and later received the Doctor of Medicine degree from Northwestern University. He completed specialty training in Orthopaedic Surgery at the University of Michigan Medical Center. This was followed by a fellowship in England under Professor Joseph Trueta at Oxford University. He was founding chairman of the Department of Orthopaedic Surgery at the School of Medicine, Texas Tech University Health Sciences Center. He is now retired.